"As a writer, I know from experienc[e] ... creative process can be, but Mark M[atousek] ... to make that potential fully conscious. A great resource for anyone wishing to develop a holistic and healing approach to writing."

> —**Sharon Salzberg**, author of *Lovingkindness* and
> *Real Happiness*

"Making sense of our lives through reflective writing is a research-established way of cultivating well-being in your life. As a scientist and clinician, I find Mark Matousek's reflections and life-changing insights in this marvelous book to be filled with timeless wisdom and practical advice. Empowering you to integrate new understandings of the past into a liberating awareness of the present, the suggestions in this helpful volume enable you to free yourself to live the life you deserve. Let Mark be your guide in this transformative book as you journey to the depths of your mind to nurture a new way of being with yourself and with others."

> —**Daniel J. Siegel, MD**, clinical professor at the David
> Geffen School of Medicine at UCLA, executive director
> at Mindsight Institute, and *New York Times* bestselling
> author of *Mind*

"In *Writing to Awaken*, Mark Matousek invites you onto a direct path of self-inquiry and spiritual realization. Mark is a masterful and loving guide: his wisdom teachings and brilliantly conceived questions will enable you to dissolve the coverings and open to life-changing truth. You don't need skill in writing to partake; all that's required is the longing to awaken your heart."

> —**Tara Brach**, author of *Radical Acceptance* and *True Refuge*

"In *Writing to Awaken*, Mark Matousek is a wise and caring guide who, like the early Eastern masters, offers insights as tools to free and build your life with. Filled with powerful stories and revealing exercises, this book opens the craft of writing as a way to dive into the art of self-reflection. It will restore meaning and change your life."

> —**Mark Nepo**, author of *The One Life We're Given* and
> *The Way Under the Way*

"*Writing to Awaken* begins with reminding readers how changing our stories transforms our lives, then leads us on a journey beginning with the self and rippling out to encompass the essence of our stories as a radical act of truth-telling. He unfolds narratives, approaches, and a rich collection of writing prompts that help us release or revise the stories that separate us from ourselves, and dwell in the stories of who we truly are. This valuable exploration helps readers become writers of their own lives, cultivating the practice, imagination, and engagement needed to awaken with compassion and courage."

> —**Caryn Mirriam-Goldberg**, 2009–2013 Poet Laureate
> of Kansas, and founder of Transformative Language
> Arts at Goddard College

"*Writing to Awaken* pulls no punches. Giving you writing prompts to serve as your scalpel, and with profound psychological and spiritual wisdom to help you step-by-step along the way, Mark Matousek invites you to dive into the depths of your life experience to explore the fundamental question: *Who am I?* This book is a solid road map for the soul, and it puts you squarely in the driver's seat."

> —**Roger Housden**, speaker, writing guide, and author of
> twenty-three books, including the best-selling *Ten Poems*
> *to Change Your Life* and *Dropping the Struggle*

"Mark Matousek unveils the path of writing as revelation. This is a beautiful book, one that will inspire writers, and really all of us, to take the pen in hand and look deeply into the human heart and into the world."

—**Roshi Joan Halifax**, abbot at Upaya Zen Center

"*Writing to Awaken* is a brilliant, practical application of expressive writing research. In his characteristically frank, accessible, and lucid language, Mark Matousek guides readers through four passages of self-exploration, providing dozens of writing prompts and examples to help readers dive deeper into their own self-discovery. Always gentle and mindfully compassionate, Matousek makes a significant contribution to the literature of writing to heal. I strongly recommend this book for those who desire to learn about the power of language to change and to discover a new, authentic way of living."

—**John F. Evans**, executive director of Wellness & Writing Connections, author of *Wellness & Writing Connections*, and coauthor with James W. Pennebaker of *Expressive Writing*

"One of Mark Matousek's great gifts to the expressive writing literature is his sensitivity to the nuances of life stories. In particular, his approach to shadow material—those dark canyons within that we're often reluctant to bring to light—is an awakening that offers healing to many readers and writers."

—**Kathleen Adams, LPC**, director of the Center for Journal Therapy, author of *Journal to the Self*, and coauthor with Deborah Ross of *Your Brain on Ink*

TESTIMONIALS

"Mark Matousek's writing instruction is transformative. His classes will change the ways in which you examine your life, and how you think about yourself as a writer. He approaches your work with a deep sense of empathy, allowing him to help you tell your story in your voice. Mark's insight, imagination, and precise instruction will push your writing in incredible directions, both creatively and technically. Mark not only recognized that I had the makings of a book, but his mentorship at every step of the process empowered me to bring the project to fruition. No matter what stage of the process you are at, time spent with Mark will yield extraordinary results."

—**Libuse Binder**, author of *Ten Ways to Change the World in Your Twenties*

"I never thought I was a writer, nor did I even attempt writing, until a friend kept at me to take Mark's workshops. Being a stubborn person who resists before plunging into anything challenging that ends up being just what I needed, I resisted for some time. Thank goodness I finally took the plunge. The workshops have been transformative for me. I found myself delving deeply into aspects of my life and digging up memories I thought were long gone. As a result, I believe that I have become a more open person and a better friend, not to mention a good writer. I am forever grateful to Mark for his time, his insights, and his ability to put his finger on each person's pulse in such a way that we all learn, not only from him but from each other. He is truly a remarkable man and a great teacher."

—**Philippa Wehle**, professor emerita of French and drama studies at the State University of New York at Purchase

Writing to Awaken

A JOURNEY OF TRUTH, TRANSFORMATION & SELF-DISCOVERY

MARK MATOUSEK

REVEAL PRESS

AN IMPRINT OF NEW HARBINGER PUBLICATIONS

Publisher's Note

Distributed in Canada by Raincoast Books

Copyright © 2017 by Mark Matousek
     Reveal Press
     An imprint of New Harbinger Publications, Inc.
     5674 Shattuck Avenue
     Oakland, CA 94609
     www.newharbinger.com

Cover design by Amy Shoup

Acquired by Ryan Buresh

Edited by Jennifer Holder

All Rights Reserved

FSC
www.fsc.org
MIX
Paper from responsible sources
FSC® C011935

Library of Congress Cataloging-in-Publication Data on file

19 18 17

10 9 8 7 6 5 4 3 2 1 First Printing

When you tell the truth, your story changes.

When your story changes, your life is transformed.

Contents

Foreword   *vii*

Introduction   *1*

Part One: Who Am I?

1   Lifting the Veil   *9*

2   Touching the Shadow   *27*

3   Your True Face   *45*

Part Two: Exploring the Story

4   Demons at the Gate   *63*

5   The Question of Meaning   *81*

6   Love Invents Us   *95*

Part Three: Dropping the Mask

7   Social Persona   *113*

8   Learning from Loss   *129*

9   The Wisdom of Intention   *143*

Part Four: Awakening

10   Awakening Genius   *159*

11   Meeting the Sacred   *177*

12   Begin Again   *193*

Acknowledgments   *212*

Bibliography   *213*

Foreword

Mark Matousek's *Writing to Awaken* is a gift to the world. An engaging process of self-inquiry guided by just the right questions, it is perhaps the most effective of all spiritual practices. Since it bypasses dogma and doctrine, it is available to anyone who wants to heal, grow, and connect with their authentic self.

When I was a child and magic was afoot, the word *abracadabra* was synonymous with the power of manifestation. I could wave my magic wand over Doris the princess doll, or Boris the stuffed panda, and practically feel them come to life under the gravitas of the spell. Later in life, as a Harvard-trained scientist and researcher in the field of mind-body medicine, I discovered that abracadabra is more than magic-speak or a song by the Steve Miller Band. These Aramaic words mean, "I will create as I speak."

Tell a story. Believe the story. And voilà! It manifests in your cells, your brain, your heart, your behavior, and the choices you make...or don't. We embody our stories quite literally, as these days we have the brain scans and hormonal assays to prove it. Mark Matousek, who is a writer rather than a scientist, knows this as well. He sometimes refers to us humans as *Homo Narrans*—the storytelling species. Stories slay and stories heal. Their transformative magic resides in our ability to identify them, learn from them, and—when necessary—change them.

I have always loved stories, which explains in part why I became a psychologist as well as a scientist. Listening to a client's story is a sacred act. Each one is a distillation of fact and feeling, an elixir that can sometimes be a poison, and other times a medicine. The nursery rhyme claiming that "sticks and stones can break my bones, but words can never hurt me," is way off target.

Words have the power to create our world. We have stories, but we are not our stories. A crisis often turns out to be an opportunity. When the light of awareness turns on through self-inquiry, a childhood belief may evaporate like dew in the sun. When the curtain of old beliefs is pulled back, we become like Dorothy in *The Wizard of Oz*. We can see past the smoke and mirrors, which enables us to take our own power back.

As Mark explains, we are always inventing ourselves through story. When we become conscious of that and are willing to write down our experiences truthfully, we can inquire deeply as both participant and observer. With even a tad of compassionate perspective, our inner and outer worlds will slowly, but surely, shift on their axes. We can finally become who we really are underneath all the layers of sediment that have accumulated in the course of our lifetime.

In the winter of 2016, Mark and I were both facilitating workshops at a retreat center in Nosara, Costa Rica. Not a bad gig in the middle of the winter. Mark's program had the same title as this book, *Writing to Awaken*. In an interesting synchronicity, mine was called *Writing Down the Light*. Since we taught sessions on different days, I was able to attend some of Mark's classes. They were masterful. He knows what questions to ask and why it's important to ask them. Each writing prompt elicited a deep and thoughtful silence in the room, and within me. The only sound was pens on paper.

At mealtimes, stories of insight, pain, and wonder abounded. Yes, there is often pain involved in telling the truth. But it's transient, as opposed to the pain of living a lifetime with beliefs and opinions about yourself and others that are much smaller than the majesty of our real, authentic selves. The final morning in Costa Rica, Mark and I officially met for the first time at the breakfast table. I felt unabashed hero worship. "He is a *real* writer," I thought to myself breathlessly. My favorite memoir of all time is his book, *Sex Death Enlightenment*. It is raw and true, scalding and funny, transcendent and thought provoking. When we met over omelets and papaya, my story was that I was a scientist and a psychologist, but certainly not a real writer. While it's true that I have written sixteen books, one of them a *New York Times* bestseller, I have always viewed my own writing as utilitarian. It's a means to an end, but certainly and unequivocally *not* real writing.

Perhaps you harbor the same unfounded myth about yourself. This is a book about writing. What if you can't do this? What if you fail? The truth is that you can't fail to develop insight and freedom when you actually sit down and work through the forty-eight lessons in this book, each one fascinating and masterfully crafted. No one is checking your work for syntax. There is no need to be clever or right. The only requirement is to tell the truth. As Mark says with an economy of words, the kind of words that distill years of spiritual practice: "When you tell the truth, your story changes. When your story changes, your life is transformed."

Several of the books I've written are also about spiritual practice. At different times in my life as a scientist, psychologist, mother, and lover, I've been immersed in Jungian psychology, Buddhism, mystical Christianity, shamanism, kabbalistic Judaism, and various forms of meditation and ceremony. Each practice has revealed another facet of the sacred. But self-inquiry, which lies at the heart of the journey you are about to embark upon, has been the most transformative—and the most gentling. Perhaps the simplest and most profound definition of the sacred I've ever read comes from this book: "The sacred connects us to what is most tender, expansive, and loving in us." This is what awakening actually feels like.

Mark has given us a superb, experiential guide for the journey of a lifetime. It's with real and humble pleasure that I give you this little pep talk called a "foreword." Read, write, and rejoice in the beauty of this amazing and mysterious gift of life.

—Joan Borysenko, PhD

Introduction

I started to write compulsively when I was in the second grade: journals filled with secret thoughts and shameful truths that I could tell no one. Many writers begin this way, turning inward as children to look for answers they can't find around them. These notebooks were my confessional, the place where I could reveal my true feelings and try to make sense of myself and the world.

I always felt better after I wrote. No matter how anxious, confused, or unsettled, my mind was clarified by writing. It was like flipping on a light in a darkened room; with words to describe what was blocking my way, suddenly I could see my way forward. Language helped me navigate my inner world—I no longer felt helpless or trapped. Afterward, I could reread what I'd written and locate clues about who I was, what I was thinking, and why this person inside me was so drastically different from what others saw.

This difference came as a revelation. The voice pouring out of me onto the page, separating truth from lies, was my fearless and natural self. This self was hidden behind a mask, a fictional story that I called "me." This mask wasn't me by a long shot, however. Writing freely, without disguise, the gap between the mask and truth—between story and self—became glaringly obvious. Odd as this disconnect was at first, I realized that it was the gateway to freedom. Through it, a message emerged loud and clear: *I am not my story.* This life-changing truth has defined my work as a memoirist, teacher, and spiritual seeker over the course of thirty years.

What does it mean to say "I am not my story?" Students ask me this all the time. "Are you saying that what happened to me didn't happen?" Of course not. "Are you calling me a liar, like I'm making these things up?" Not at all. What I'm acknowledging—along with a vast majority of psychologists, physicists, and spiritual teachers—is that what we believe to be real is not reality. The mind creates stories out of things that happen and composes a character they happen to. We then take these false stories for fact and live as if they are the actual truth.

We do this because we are Homo Narrans, the storytelling species, the only animal in all of existence that creates a conceptualized self. We invent ourselves at every moment—connecting the dots, developing plot lines, revising scenes, replaying old dramas—by composing a solid narrative with this fictional self at the center. We fully believe that our story is real, which is why when I tell students that every life is a work of fiction, they quite often feel existential confusion. Luckily, this confusion doesn't last long.

Seeing that the story isn't ourselves is a quantum leap in self-realization and the starting point of a whole new life. Engaging with that conscious life is what this book is about. *Writing to Awaken* is a journey of self-awareness deepened by the exploration of the stories you tell yourself and the masks you wear in the world. The transformational power of this writing practice continues to amaze me after all these years. The radical act of telling the truth awakens us *automatically.* When we write down our story, we become the witness, and this objective distance brings an *aha!* as the character we believed to be solid reveals itself as a narrative construct. As we move together through this journey, you'll come to understand this better. For now, just remember a simple message that will make the way clearer as you progress.

When you tell the truth, your story changes.

When your story changes, your life is transformed.

Why is telling the truth so radical? Because we rarely do so completely in social life. As socialized animals, we're taught to hide our feelings, to protect reputations, conventions, and interests. We're liars of necessity, fear, and convenience. Imagine if everyone told the whole truth—regardless of the consequences. It would be a brutal nightmare! To avoid incrimination and cruelty, we opt instead for versions of the truth, euphemisms, half-lies, and tidied-up candor. Though we're *mostly* honest, most of the time, civilized life calls for reticence and cooperation breeds compromise.

Then there is the matter of shame. We tolerate such heavy loads of it that revealing the truth can seem menacing, as if uncensored honesty might wreak havoc on our carefully manicured lives. Shame tends to keep us dishonest and silent, sitting on our secrets, trapped in the dark. That is why finally telling the truth—in writing, therapy, or a church confessional—has such a catalytic effect. We're awakened by its unmistakable sound, like the pealing of a bell. Once we've rung that bell, it can't be unrung. We're called on to live with what we know since the fiction of self no longer traps us. We understand why we have felt inauthentic—in subtle as well as obvious ways. Wiping away the mask of lies, we reveal our true face in the mirror through writing, often for the first time.

The benefits of expressive writing are incalculable. They include psychological empowerment, emotional healing, social intelligence, increased well-being, creative growth, and a spiritual awareness that keeps us rooted in the life we're living. Research has shown that as little as fifteen minutes of expressive writing a day can markedly improve physical and mental health. Unlike journaling, expressive writing requires that we do more than simply report the facts of our experience or free-associate on any random subject that comes to mind. The research of psychologist James W. Pennebaker reveals that in order for writing to be transformative, we must include our thoughts, emotions, beliefs, and insights about our experience if we hope to reap the benefits. Pennebaker's studies have shown that when subjects approach writing in this way, the practice can boost the immune system, reduce the need for psychotherapy, lower stress, and even accelerate physical healing.

The journey in *Writing to Awaken* is divided into four parts that each lead to the next. Along the way, I will offer reflections and many examples from students who have participated in my classes. While their names have been changed, their stories are real.

Part One starts with a question: who am I? This is the departure point for traditions of self-inquiry that precede even Socrates with his ancient maxim to "know thyself." You'll investigate your personal creation myth, explore the contents of your psychological shadow, uncover the nature of family attachments, and be introduced to the witnessing awareness that allows you to observe yourself clearly and gain insight from what you see.

Part Two explores your stories themselves, revealing the cast of saboteurs that block you internally, as well as how shame operates in your life, how you relate to purpose and meaning, and how love shapes the person you are.

Part Three considers your public persona, questioning things like performance, intention, power, control, and how you may be hindered by ambivalence or lack of focus.

In Part Four, you'll learn how to reap the gifts of transformation, reveal the sacredness and spirit in an awakened life, and harness the power of the original genius that is uncovered in this truth-telling process.

In total, there are forty-eight lessons contained in these sections. It's best to complete these lessons in sequence, taking all the time you need for each one. At the end of each lesson, you'll find a series of in-depth writing prompts for you to choose from. It's advisable, but not necessary, that you respond to all prompts, choosing any sequence that works for you. Trust your instincts and write about the questions that have the deepest resonance. You can always revisit these lessons in the future to explore questions that you skip.

Trust your own rhythm and the pace that suits you best. Deadlines can be helpful as long as they're realistic, but do your best not to turn this into a writing marathon. Take your time with the questions, allow yourself to dive deep, but resist including everything that pops into your head. I recommend a maximum length of one-thousand words per response, which translates to four, double-spaced, typewritten pages. This word limit will help you distill the writing and train your mind not to wander too much.

Whenever possible, avoid throat-clearing and lengthy prefacing of your responses. Instead, go to the heart of what you want to say. You'll notice how evasive your mind can become when asked direct questions, particularly around sensitive subjects. Like all forms of awakening practice, writing requires mindfulness. Just as we bring our attention back to the breath during meditation, you learn to observe the wandering mind without excessive control, and gently return your focus to the question at hand.

Some writing days will be better than others, as happens with any ongoing practice. Expect to meet your own saboteurs along the way. Truth telling frequently calls up resistance; in fact, you will typically know you're approaching a breakthrough when you feel discomfort. That's when it is most important to stick with the practice. The more you write, the more comfortable you'll become with the discomfort of revealing dangerous knowledge and saying unsayable things.

If you find yourself feeling nothing when you write, or notice that you're getting bored with a topic, see those as signs that you're not taking risks. Pause and ask yourself: "What am I avoiding?" "What scares me here?" "What is niggling at me to get onto the page?" Allow yourself to follow these detours without losing sight of the question at hand. They can lead to discoveries you did not intend to make. As the philosopher Martin Buber reminds us, "Every journey has a secret destination of which the traveler is unaware." This holds true for the writing adventure as well. By using the lessons offered in this book as points of departure, and the prompts as invitations to destinations unknown, you'll stay open to what is below the surface of your conscious mind.

Remember that writing is only half of the process. After you've responded to a question, set it aside for a day. Then reread it. While you may have gained insight through your initial response to the prompt, it's when you notice the gaps in what you've written—between what is true and your story about it—that transformation happens. Allow yourself the time to write about what you noticed during the review and to fill in any blanks. This close attention to your responses will deepen your insight. You'll become less afraid of the witness's perspective and what it reveals. You'll see that the fears themselves are stories, which dissipate when you face them head on.

Although our medium is writing, you don't need any writing skill for this practice to work. Literary talent is irrelevant here, and so are grammar, syntax, and elegant prose. The strengths you need are courage, transparency, commitment to the truth, and a sincere desire to transcend your story. I've guided thousands of students around the world through these lessons and am continually astonished by the cathartic power of *Writing to Awaken* and its lasting effects on people's lives. I invite you to embark on this journey, dive into your own deep waters, and find out who you really are.

Part One

WHO AM I?

1 Lifting the Veil

As you will soon learn, your personal story is not the whole truth. We use narratives to explain ourselves and the world, but these interpretations are subjective and changeable. Each of us composes a creation myth based on the stories we're told by our parents and family. This myth is combined with childhood experience to form the building blocks of personal identity. As you write and see that ideas about yourself are constructed from stories that are essentially used to connect various dots into a tidy picture, you realize that self-image is a work of fiction. Acknowledging this gap between story and truth is the first step to psychological and spiritual freedom. This is how awakening begins.

A CASE OF MISTAKEN IDENTITY

As a child, you believe what you're told. If your parents tell you that you are "Sally," you assume that you are Sally—an identity with a name. This identity forms an image in your mind and this image is what you think of as you. As this image moves through life, it imagines that it is living a story, and that this story and the image are one and the same. This is how you came to confuse what is truth and what is fiction.

There's an allegory that captures this universal human tendency. A group of tigers leaves a cub behind in the forest by mistake. The cub is found by a herd of sheep. They take the tiger in as one of their own. They teach it to bleat like a sheep and walk like a sheep and eat grass like a good sheep should. Years later, an adult tiger sees this half-grown tiger prancing around like an overgrown lamb. The tiger takes the youth by the tail and pulls him to a pond where he can see his own reflection in the water. For the first time, the tiger sees what he really is. Then the older tiger teaches him to roar. At first, all he can do is bleat, but slowly a more powerful sound begins in the back of his throat. Finally, after weeks of practice, the young tiger lets out the great roar of freedom.

Even though we're not aware of it, this is how you and I spend our lives. We're taught to see ourselves as sheep: small, domesticated, herd-bound creatures defined by the stories our parents tell us. These stories comprise a self-image with seemingly ironclad legitimacy. Once we start a process of self-inquiry, however, we realize that our life is based on a case of mistaken identity.

This happened to a student of mine. Cleo had been adopted at birth by an elderly couple, Polish Jews who barely survived World War II. They kept her adoption a secret. Kind but smothering, caring but paranoid, they communicated their deep anxieties to Cleo with toxic lessons about being a scapegoat and a social outcast. Cleo grew into a lonely, withdrawn woman, who struggled with her parents' legacy even after their deaths. Then one day, her mother's sister called and said she had something she needed to tell Cleo. Cleo drove to the suburbs and learned that her parents were not her birth parents—that Cleo wasn't even Jewish. Instead, she was the daughter of a Swedish woman the family knew who couldn't afford to raise another baby. In the midst of an identity crisis, Cleo took my online writing class with a single, obsessive query in mind: "who am I?" With her family story taken away, Cleo described feeling more alone than ever before. "Suddenly, the floor dropped out and I'm left hanging by nothing, barely a thread. That's how it feels. I have no roots. I don't belong anywhere. No one knows who I am. It's the most arid, painful feeling. My story wasn't that great, but at least it was mine. Now what do I have?"

I encouraged Cleo to explore her own question and gave her these prompts: "When you look in the mirror now, with the story taken away, what do you see? Is anything different? If so, what?" A week passed before Cleo finally responded.

I didn't want to do this at first. When I finally got to a mirror, looked at myself, and asked your questions, I stared into my own eyes to make myself be really honest. And that's when I saw it: nothing had changed. Not a single thing was different now that I knew they weren't my parents. It was a story of my own, an idea of myself. Who I am is still here. The story has nothing to do with it.

Cleo's epiphany changed her perspective. After grieving this loss of innocence and letting go of a family she thought was hers, Cleo realized that she was also free of a lifetime of loneliness and oppression—the weighty heritage they had given her. Though Cleo still loved the people who'd raised her, she was no longer trapped in their story. She knew she was not that story. What had appeared to be a void suddenly revealed itself as open space, in which Cleo could discover what she wanted and what came naturally to her. By the end of the course, she was planning a move to Florida to pursue her secret fantasy of getting a degree in hospitality.

"My parents would have been horrified of all those strangers," Cleo wrote in her final submission. "But nothing could be stranger than what already happened. I feel like I'm ready for anything."

Like Cleo, we're all tigers behaving as sheep, avoiding the truth of our own reflection. We're cut off from our roar of freedom. But the moment we get ourselves to the mirror, or the blank page, this starts to change if we're willing to be honest about what we see. Before you begin to write, consider the core insights of this lesson.

Core Insights

☐ The identity we were given by our parents forms an image that creates a story as we move through life. We believe that our image and story are one and the same, which is how we come to confuse truth with fiction.

☐ When we start the process of self-inquiry, we come to see that this story is a case of mistaken identity.

☐ Until we look past our stories, we're cut off from our authentic voice.

☐ If we're willing to be honest about what we see in the mirror, we can change our story and break free from limiting beliefs.

Dive Deeper

These deepening practices will help you begin a process of self-recognition. Take your time as you move through these writing prompts and be as truthful as possible. Try not to hold anything back as you explore the implications of having a mistaken identity.

- Describe yourself as a child from your parents' points of view. How did they see you? Who did they want you to be? What story did they tell you about who you were? In what ways did that narrative help to form your identity?

- In what ways does this story contradict who you really are? How is your life a case of mistaken identity?

- Describe an experience of surprising yourself with uncharacteristic behavior. What did this teach you about your story?

- What aspects of your mistaken identity are most challenging for you to let go? Why are you attached to particular falsehoods? Be specific.

Now that you recognize the limitations of your given identity, you can begin to free yourself of those limitations. This leads you to the next step in self-discovery: opening the door to your secrets.

TELLING SECRETS

At first, it may be difficult to admit that your story is constructed from false information. Every life is a patchwork of secrets, half-truths, cover-ups, shams, and disguises. The most authentic among us have hidden compartments, shadowy corners, and contradictions we keep under wraps for fear of destroying our public image. As you disclose these secrets to yourself, you come to peel back layers of falsehood and reveal yourself as you truly are: a complex individual with myriad dimensions and conflicting needs. As you do this, you can integrate these clandestine parts into a more harmonious whole.

This medicine can be a hard pill to swallow because we like to see ourselves as being transparent and don't want to admit that we have secrets. Students often reject the suggestion that they are hiding anything. "I'm an open book," they protest. "What you see is what you get!" Ironically, these very objectors are very often the most secretive, deceptive people in class. Their exaggerated need to be trusted and seen as having no secrets is frequently a dead give-away that the opposite is true.

I ran into this paradox when Antoinette joined my private writing group. Effusive and outspoken, Antoinette was a psychotherapist with a razor-sharp mind and a rollicking laugh. At forty-five, she'd been through analysis herself and had a thriving private practice working with trauma survivors. Upon hearing that the topic of the week was telling secrets, Antoinette claimed to have nothing to write about. "I've told them all," she announced to the class, "I have nothing left to hide." I asked her if that was really true. Her cheerful expression turned querulous as Antoinette replied, "I should know." I suggested that she dig a bit deeper. If she came up empty-handed, and actually had no secrets to tell, then she could use this time to write about how it feels to be free of secrets and the ways this impacts her life. The following week, Antoinette came to the group looking upset. She accused me of trespassing her boundaries and reminded me that, unlike her, I am not a licensed health care professional. Her message seemed to be: *How dare you question my integrity?* I reassured Antoinette, who eventually calmed down and agreed to revisit the question of secrecy. When she showed up for our next meeting, Antoinette was still upset—but not at me. "I have something to read to the group," she told us. Here's part of what Antoinette read.

> *My husband and I have an open marriage. We chose this*
> *arrangement years ago after he admitted to having an*
> *affair. We kept this quiet and didn't tell family or friends,*
> *mostly to be discreet for the kids, rather than out of shame*
> *or secrecy. Polyamory has worked for us very well; no lies,*
> *no guilt, no sneaking around behind each other's backs.*
> *I've been telling myself that it was all good—I love Dave,*
> *but I'm not in love with him. He's the father of my children*
> *and I'd do anything to give them the security they need.*
> *But lately, this has been changing for me, not only because*
> *I don't want to sleep with Dave anymore, but also because*
> *I'm falling in love with the man I'm dating. That's a*
> *lie—I'm already madly in love and he feels the same way*
> *about me. It's driving me crazy, I'm very unhappy, and I've*
> *been lying to Dave for months about why I'm so distant*
> *and where I've been going on weekends. I'm starting to*
> *hate myself for this, even though Dave started it. Now, I'm*
> *up against the wall in a room I never wanted to be in.*

Antoinette was visibly upset as she read this to the group. The pretense of having no secrets had dropped. Suddenly she was simply a woman in love: vulnerable, confused, and tender. I encouraged Antoinette to write about this love, her connection to this man, the dishonesty within her marriage. Could she live with this duplicity? Antoinette explored these questions in the following weeks and decided to be honest with her husband. It turned out that he had fallen in love with the woman he was dating, but didn't know how to tell Antoinette. She was able to write about her relief and how they planned to integrate this information into their marriage. The last time I saw Antoinette, she seemed more comfortable inside her own skin. We laughed together over her previous protestations. "I was lying to myself," she said.

That's the important point. It's not necessary to share your secrets with others, like Antoinette did. What matters is that you admit them to yourself, so that you aren't putting blinders on your own awareness and duping yourself into believing a false self-image. It's extraordinary how adept we are at self-deception and keeping the truth in conveniently hidden compartments. We're masters of the partial reveal. We add the spin so that everyone else's view of us remains favorable.

As you write down your secrets, you see how these insidious narratives, the ones you keep hidden, are running your life and prompting your choices. It's important to be candid with yourself because your secrets are clues to what needs healing and can point out the direction in which you want to grow.

Crisis can be useful for this as well, as it cracks our stories open. In the midst of crisis, we're less defended and our secrets come closer to the surface. We can't be quite as opaque. As challenging as this can be, it's an invitation to tell the truth. That's why people who survive a major crisis are often the most enlightened among us: energized, open, and engaged. They have excavated their own secrets, cover-ups, and self-deceptions, and are no longer strangers to themselves. There are treasures hidden in the shadows and finding them is part of this journey. You can claim what you have kept in the dark, including your own hidden gifts. The writing you do in this lesson will help you open the door to your secret world.

Core Insights

☐ We may find it difficult to admit that our story is made up of secrets, half-truths, cover-ups, shams, and disguises that we keep under wraps for fear of destroying our public image.

☐ When we peel back the layers of falsehood, we reveal who we truly are and we are able to integrate our clandestine parts into a more harmonious whole.

☐ Our secrets are clues about what needs healing and can point out the direction in which we want to grow.

☐ Crisis can be useful because it cracks our story open. We become less defended and our secrets come closer to the surface.

Dive Deeper

When you allow yourself to open the door to your secrets, you discover a hidden world full of valuable information. You see that one secret leads to the next, so that the more truthful you allow yourself to be, the more clandestine material is revealed. These prompts will help you uncover these secrets.

• Tell a secret that you've never shared with anyone. This secret can be significant or trivial. What matters is that it has been clandestine.

• What is your greatest source of shame? When did this shame story begin and how does it affect your life?

• Describe how secrecy helps you feel safe. How does it protect your reputation? How does it maintain the appearance of integrity?

- What would your closest friends and family be most surprised to learn about you if you told the whole truth? Be specific.

By acknowledging your secret lives, you bring attention to seminal questions inside yourself that deepen self-inquiry and throw light on your persona. The issues you raise have roots in your earliest beliefs about identity and the family into which you were born.

THE CREATION MYTH

Each of us is born into a story, a family saga that predates our subjective narrative and foreshadows the person we will become. Although we are individuals, we are also part of a greater whole, a family tree with roots reaching back to the first human beings who walked the earth. As characters in this long-running play, we inherit all that has come before us. Our blood is rich with information. Our bodies hold secrets, clues, and stories accessible through intuition and by reaching imaginatively into the past.

Writing is an act of the imagination. This is important to understand because when we dream back in time to describe things that happened long ago, imagination enables us to recreate from memory. We can make stories out of fragments of what we remember. In our mind, these stories take the place of what happened—meaning that *how* we remember things is more important than *what* really happened.

This is particularly true when we look at childhood, that long-ago time when we were at our most impressionable, as well as our most ignorant. As psychologist James Hillman reminds us, "Our lives are determined less by our childhood than by the traumatic way we have learned to remember our childhoods." That's why understanding your creation myth is so helpful. It reveals what you believe about your own genesis, the story you've imagined to explain how you came into the world.

With Cleo's story, we saw how important a creation myth is to a sense of self. After she learned of her adoption, Cleo's identity seemed to go to pieces and she was left wondering how she could create a present with so little information about her past and where she'd come from. While Cleo came to recognize this loss as an opportunity to free herself from one painful narrative, she couldn't help imagining a different, potentially problematic story as the child of an unmarried, non-Jewish woman and a mystery father she'd never know. Like nature, the mind hates a vacuum, so when facts are unavailable the imagination reflexively fills in the blanks. What determines the sturdiness of your narrative structure is *how* you fill in these memory gaps.

I learned this when I wrote a book about finding my own absent father. Growing up without a dad, I felt that half of my own story was missing, as if part of me had disappeared the night I last saw him when I was four years old—part of me that was forever lost. My hunger to find him forty years later grew out of my desire to finish the story, to build a foundation for my life that felt less wobbly and incomplete. The detective never found my father but that didn't matter much, in the end, because the search itself prompted me to write, and writing revealed what needed attention. In my case, I needed to pay attention to love, the absence of love between my parents, and how I imagined this absence affected my own ability to love. One of the things I wrote down was my own creation myth.

By exploring my imagined beginnings, I was able to uncover some surprising beliefs about the people who were my parents and my own genetic inheritance. In this story, it's the mother who's absent and the father who's left wondering where she has gone. He wants her more than she wants him. She disappears to a place where he is not allowed to go—an emotional place where he can't find her. It was impossible for me not to notice how closely this mirrored my own experience as the only son of this distant mother. I imagined that when I entered my mother's body, she had already drifted someplace else. When I reflected on what I'd written, I saw how this legacy of conflict and emotional mismatch reflected itself in my life story. I'd swallowed this myth of my own creation from cues that were largely preverbal. This had led to a tragic-romantic life narrative in which I was looking for the right one but never finding that relationship. I believed that I had a conflicted heart but in fact it was the story in my mind that was the problem.

When you allow yourself to write *imaginatively* about this moment of creation, drawing on what you've been told about your parents' relationship, you're able to access elements of your unspoken narrative that prompt insight and emotional healing. Let yourself dream back to that primal moment and uncover the myth that's waiting there. You may be surprised by what you find as you write about your imagined beginnings. To help get you started, here is what kicked off my writing, from my book *The Boy He Left Behind*.

> *Try to imagine your own conception. Conjure the primal scene in your mind, your parents' bodies thrashing together. What are they thinking? How attentive are they to each other? Does she already know that you've entered her life, or has she drifted somewhere else? Have you ever wondered what she was thinking at the moment you first took root inside her, and whether your mother's hazy thoughts might have been your first musings too? Whether her mood, and your father's as well, their histories, hopes, and true intentions, the wealth or lack of love between them, the dreams they shared or would never share, might have affected the seed being planted, and the shape of who you became? How can we know when memory begins?*

Core Insights

☐ Each of us is born into a story, a family saga that predates subjective narrative and foreshadows the people we will become.

☐ We are part of a family tree with roots reaching back to the first human beings who walked the earth, inheriting all that has come before us.

☐ Writing is an act of the imagination, which enables us to recreate stories from fragments of memories. *How* we remember things is often more important than *what* actually happened.

☐ When we write the story of our creation, we're able to access elements of our unspoken narrative that prompt insight and emotional healing.

Dive Deeper

You're now ready to explore a creation myth on your own. Allow your imagination free rein as you give voice to this personal story and how it has shaped your beliefs and self-image.

• Imagine the moment of your own conception. Describe the atmosphere in detail, including your parents' emotional, spiritual, and physical lives, as well as their relationship.

• What is the connection between your self-image and this imagined union? How has your parent's legacy impacted your story? Do you see yourself as a product of love? Accident? Obligation? Confusion? Be specific.

• Do you identify more with your mother or your father? When did this alignment begin? What are its implications? How has it affected your bond with the other parent?

• If it was possible for children to choose their parents, why might you have chosen yours? What aspects of your soul's journey were satisfied by these particular people?

The antecedents to your life narrative—and the self-image you have created—are connected to your creation myth in mysterious and significant ways. Once you recognize how this self-image formed, you become the storyteller, not the story. You realize that you are the dreamer, not the dream. This leads to the next important step in awakening to who you are.

SELF-IMAGE

Self-image is the portrait we carry in our head, representing the person we imagine ourselves to be. This self-image bears a scant resemblance to how others see us or to our actual appearance. It's a distorted, subjective view made up of stories, beliefs, emotions, desires, biases, and insecurities that have little factual basis. As an inside job, self-image is entirely personal and subjective. While it may evolve over time, self-image tends to glue into place like a photograph fixed on a moving object, concealing the truth of who we are.

How does self-image become so entrenched? Through the imposition of narrative labels. Putting names to things solidifies them in our minds. For example, if you're a cautious, timid, fearful person, you might lump those all-too-human qualities into a label such as "coward." That label will take on the appearance of fact and become a defining aspect of your self-image. When labels are legitimized by groups or social stereotypes, they become broader and more intractable, like "Evangelical Christian," "welfare recipient," "disabled vet," "suburban wife," or "convicted felon." As psychological shorthand, these labels contribute to a generic picture of who we believe we are and place limits on our potential.

Richard learned this lesson the hard way. The oldest son of Japanese American immigrants, he was raised to view himself as a glorified slave to his father's ambitions. Harsh, demanding, and critical, Richard's father had grown up poor in rural Japan. He was violent toward Richard. He wanted his son to follow him into the discount jewelry business, but Richard dreamed of being a writer. This is how he introduced himself to our online class.

I'm Japanese first, my father's son second, my mother's son third, and my own person last. That's how I see myself. You don't know what it's like to be the oldest son in a Japanese family. It's is all about your role, duty, piety, ancient values. I painted myself with all of their colors, and somewhere inside, there is me: I can hear his heart beating but can't see his face.

I asked Richard to describe that heartbeat as a voice talking to him. What was it saying? He responded, "I'm suffocating, gasping for air, screaming 'Get my father off me.'" I had an image of Richard, locked in a fight to the death with his father, pinned underneath him and unable to throw him off. In Richard's story, he was forever overpowered by his father's presence and forced to subjugate his own desires. I asked him to question the details of this story, one by one, and test them against the truth. Though his feelings were undeniably real, the story was full of assumptions and labels that were not true. I invited Richard to consider this and the payoffs for believing the story. He wrote:

I started to look at the details of this image of myself. I'm not Japanese first, I'm human first. I'm not my father's son second, I'm myself second. Just writing that made me feel good. Why would I think my uniqueness is less important than my nationality or my father's big personality? This was an aha! Then I asked: what's the payoff for seeing myself this way? First of all, it lets me get angry and blame him for what's wrong in my life, for all the ways I don't feel happy. I'm a firstborn Japanese son, so that explains everything, doesn't it? I wimp out on my career. Blame my father! I chase the girl away by putting my family before her. Filial piety! This image is a good excuse to cover anything that doesn't work.

By questioning his self-image, Richard's portrait began to fall apart. He was hiding inside a self-image that allowed him to perpetuate his own fiction. But once he saw this, he could no longer let the tail (the story) wag the dog (him).

We all use self-image to rationalize our own choices: "I'm not the kind of person who..." or "Someone with my background could never do that!" We reflexively cling to these images. As long as we maintain the status quo and there are no serious threats to our self-image, we're able to maintain this fiction by pretending that we are contained by it. But when life rips away our cherished labels—as it eventually will—we're given a view of endless possibilities: "Yes, I can be the kind of person who..." We realize that, far from being limited, we are protean, shape-shifting creatures in a process of perpetual change. Instead of being a single self, we can each be a chorus of multiple voices, notes within a single, evolving chord.

"Do I contradict myself?" Walt Whitman asked in *Leaves of Grass*. "Very well then I contradict myself, / (I am large, I contain multitudes.)" So do you. Take a closer look at the chorus you have within you and how the voices in your chorus come together to form your self-image.

Core Insights

☐ Self-image is the portrait we carry in our head, representing the person we imagine ourselves to be. It's a distorted, subjective view made up of stories, beliefs, emotions, desires, biases, and insecurities that have little to no factual basis.

☐ Through the imposition of labels, we create a generic picture of who we believe we are and place limits on our potential.

☐ By questioning the details of our self-image, our portrait falls apart. We are no longer able to perpetuate our own fiction.

☐ Instead of being a single self in a fixed image, we are a chorus of multiple voices, notes within a single, evolving chord.

Dive Deeper

It's a great relief to realize that everyone's personality is made up of contradictory voices. When it comes to character or self-image, there's no such thing as complete consistency. These questions will help you understand your own contradictions and see how to make peace with your internal chorus.

- Take five minutes to describe yourself, in twenty-five words or less, to someone you've never met. Do not edit this description. When you reread the description the next day, write about the labels you used to represent yourself. What do you notice? Which don't quite fit? What vital descriptors have you left out?

- Are you able to be flexible in times of change? Or do you automatically defend your self-image? How does this habit affect the way you make choices?

- What aspects of your self-image appear to be non-negotiable? What characteristics, if lost, would cause you to stop feeling like yourself?

- Name the features in your self-image that are consistently problematic or disempowering. What do you get out of holding on to them?

Simply acknowledging the limitations of your self-image, and the falsehoods it contains, allows you to step outside that image and look around at what is true. When you do this, you realize that these true qualities have been with you all this time, hidden by a kind of shadow. As you'll see in the next chapter, "Touching the Shadow," we choose which aspects of ourselves to legitimize and which to deny out of shame or fear. Retrieving the truth from your shadow is the next step toward maturity and wholeness.

2 Touching the Shadow

Your shadow is that off-limits part of your psyche where you hide stories that cause you shame or fear. As you learn to navigate it, you'll see positive as well as negative stories concealed there, gifts as well as destructive elements. By examining falsehoods, self-deceptions, and out-and-out lies, you'll deepen your understanding of how shadow helps you survive—and blocks you from thriving if you don't investigate its contents. As a writer, it is important to have access to an inner refuge, as it offers a vantage point that is protected and stable, so you can do this deep investigation.

THE FALSEHOODS OF SELF

In the process of becoming an individual, composing a story that's ours alone, we pick and choose who we want to be—and who we absolutely don't want to be. We relegate the undesirable parts, or those we can't make sense of, to our psychological shadow, the dark side of our personal moon. In time, we come to believe that these hidden parts don't really exist if nobody (not even us) knows that they're there. The more we are able to forget our shadow, the easier our life becomes. Then one day, we look around and realize that big chunks of ourselves have gone missing, leaving us as an impostor, cut off from the truth.

This is the downside of storytelling, because there are many things we have to leave out. We can't have a story without a frame, and we can't have a frame without limitations. This psychological editing happens before we've even heard of the shadow. Every time we're punished or praised, encouraged or taunted, gifted with the fulfillment of a desire or disappointed, we decide what belongs in the light and what goes into the shadow. Depending on personality and environment, we are drawn to different styles of attracting attention and love. One child learns that when she's good, her parents shower her with affection, but when she disobeys they ignore her. Another child learns that when she's good, no one pays her the slightest attention, but when she disobeys she becomes the center of attention. These two children are likely to grow up relegating different sorts of traits to the shadow according to how these qualities are received. The principle is the same, however. We use what works and discard what doesn't in order to survive and fit in.

This makes for a lopsided internal load that grows more burdensome over time. We may not know quite what the matter is—we just know that *something* in us is causing a lot of grief. The poet Robert Bly claims that we spend the first forty years of life putting things into the shadow bag and the last forty years taking them out. It's impossible to know ourselves and reach our potential while denying so much of what is inside us. Fortunately, writing is an excellent way to remove things from that shadow bag, hold them up to the light of consideration, and reclaim what's ours to keep.

Toni attended one of my weekend workshops. She was a yoga teacher with a thriving community of followers all over the world. Gliding into class in flowing white clothes, she looked like a blond Nordic goddess. She was soft-spoken, graceful, and always smiling—an ethereal being in a room full of earthlings. The class was in awe of Toni, especially after I asked her to read her self-portrait aloud. She said, "I am a prism, a glass in the sun, containing nothing and everything. Space. Nothing can touch me, though I touch all. Transmitting light: sweet offering."

I immediately smelled a rat. Toni's self-portrait contained no shadow. The divine allusions were lyrical, but problematic. Toni seemed to be greatly invested in presenting herself as an angel of light who was barely terrestrial—which told me that there must be lots of imperfect earth-stuff hiding in her shadow bag. For a couple of weeks, she maintained this spiritual facade, writing about "the death of ego" and how it felt to be enlightened. Then, in week three, Toni's mask began to slip when the class did the "Telling Secrets" exercise. She wrote:

> *My father committed suicide when I was ten. No one told me what had happened. Mommy refused to talk about it. It took years to find out. It turns out that the year before I was born, my father had an accident in the driveway. He ran over my three-year-old brother, who I didn't even know existed, and he died in front of him. That's when Mommy got pregnant with me. They named me after little Anthony.*

In the years since that time, Toni had come to believe that her birth was part of a cosmic plan in which her soul chose to incarnate to take her brother's place, and that it was a blessing to be given this healing mission. Toni wrote, "I have always welcomed the opportunity to serve." Without questioning this belief, I asked her to write about any problems or challenges that came with this demanding task.

"I don't see them as problems," she responded, saying that viewing things that way was old-paradigm thinking. "Are you asking if there was pain? I would have to say yes. I guess my 'pain,' if that's the right word, comes from feeling badly for my parents. Not being able to make them happy. Wondering if I've completed my mission." In Toni's life story, she was the savior figure who came to earth with the sole purpose of relieving her parent's suffering and bringing light and hope to the world. To this end, she'd kept her own, very human, needs and emotions stuffed deep in her shadow bag. To ensure that her dark parts remained hidden, Toni had constructed a personality so bright that it left no room for natural human complexity, or self-doubt. I invited her to reclaim her discarded parts and offer herself the same compassion she gave so generously to others. When asked to write about who she might be without this creation story, as an ordinary little girl born into a grief-stricken family, she ran into a wall of fear. Finally, Toni was able to hypothetically describe this girl-self: "She'd be sad, I suppose. Probably confused. Scared that her mother might disappear, too. She might feel guilty that she wasn't perfect. Like 'why should I be alive instead of my brother?' I know my father wanted a son. When I write that down, I feel like crying."

As the class progressed, Toni continued to pull things out of her shadow bag. As she did so, we witnessed a visible change in her. She became more accessible, humble, and real. Toni was still beatific and unusually kind, but the angelic routine began to fade. She wrote about her longing for children, and the fears she felt about being a mother. She described a troubled relationship with her own alcoholic mother and a fear that she would never stop drinking. Toni realized she was a textbook codependent dressed in savior's clothing. By touching her shadow, Toni was experiencing a kind of spiritual maturity she had never known before, which included dropping the myth that "Nothing can touch me, though I touch all." By the end of the nine-week class, she was considering Al-Anon meetings and had enrolled in a class on tantric massage. In the final exercise, she wrote:

> *I need to come into my body. But when you have a body, you have a shadow. When you have a shadow, you have clay feet. I didn't want to feel that vulnerable. But how can you surrender to God without vulnerability? The truth is, I had to keep a distance from everyone and everything, including myself. I want to engage with my life now. I know I'm still a work in progress, but at least I'm not hiding anymore.*

That's the point. When you touch the shadow, you come out of hiding. The dark side of the moon becomes visible. As the psychologist Carl Jung wrote, "One does not become enlightened by imagining figures of light, but by making the darkness conscious." As you continue to explore your own shadow, you'll see how writing helps to illuminate the darkness, draw attention to what's been ignored, and uncover wisdom we didn't know we had.

Core Insights

☐ In the process of composing a story that suits our needs, we put our undesirable parts into our psychological shadow.

☐ The more we are able to forget our shadow, the easier our life becomes. We use what works, and discard what doesn't, in order to survive and fit in.

☐ It's impossible to know ourselves and reach our potential while denying so much of what is inside us.

☐ Writing is an excellent practice for removing things from our shadow bag and reclaiming what is ours to keep.

Dive Deeper

This is a challenging, but rewarding, step in your practice. Writing about your shadow parts can bring up pain, and also relief and clarity. Trust the process.

• What half-truths and lies do you tell on a regular basis? How does each one serve and hinder you? Who would you be without these falsehoods?

• How do fear, judgment, and insecurity lead to falsehood in your life? Be specific.

• Explore the link between falsehood and disempowerment. How do the lies you tell yourself contribute to a loss of meaning?

- How would you describe the voice of your internal censor? Whose voice is it? What does it tell you to be ashamed of?

The shadow is bound to surprise you as you continue to explore its contents. There are so many secrets, and so many gifts. Let's look more closely at what the shadow is made of and how it operates in our lives.

THE SHADOW KNOWS

In Jungian psychology, the shadow refers to unconscious aspects of self that our personality doesn't know how to deal with. To make sense of ourselves and create a comfortable daylight image, we habitually shadow the parts of ourselves that are threatening, embarrassing, confusing, vulnerable-making, wounded, or are even cruel, venal, or dishonest. The shadow is full of everything that we deny about ourselves: the things that we don't want to face, the places that scare us, the qualities that are threatening or shameful. This includes our demons.

At the same time, the shadow includes positive things that we may suppress in order to toe the line, conform, and create this life that we have. Let's say that you're an artist at heart, but your parents wanted you to become a lawyer or do something that would enable you to make a secure living. So you took a cautious professional path and suppressed the things in yourself that were creative, free, wild, and passionate; things that may have thrown you off your straight-and-narrow course, had you let them come into your life.

The problem is, when you suppress things into the shadow, they often come out in unhealthy ways. Addiction is a common, sideways expression of the shadow. Jung called addiction "a prayer gone awry" because it's often the prayer we have for ourselves that is thwarted by addiction. When we suppress the intimate truths of our desires and longings, we may fill their voids with destructive semi-pleasures. But because they are driven by unexplored parts or our shadow, they diminish us rather than enlarge us, and keep us on the surface of our own existence.

While the shadow is adaptive and helps us survive, we must examine its contents if we are to grow. "Everyone carries a shadow, and the less it is embodied in the individual's conscious life, the blacker and denser it is," Jung explained. Just as shamans are trained to pass through spiritual darkness before emerging with second sight, we too must learn to pass through the shadow in the process of self-realization. Eve was a widow who lost her beloved husband suddenly in a boating accident. In the aftermath of his premature death, Eve attempted to take her life twice and shut herself into her lonely house on a rural lake. She refused counseling, medication, get-away vacation offers, and anything meant to raise her spirits. Instead, Eve stayed where she was, put her life on hold, and sank into melancholy. The one activity that held her attention was organizing her late husband's paintings. She hoped that by touching his canvases, she would feel she was touching him.

I suggested Eve explore the stories she held about being alone. It seemed there were two griefs pulling her down: the natural grief over her husband's death and an equally strong grief over having her life story taken away. She was being forced to explore life as a single woman—a prospect that filled her with dread. The testimony she sent me confirmed my suspicions. She wrote:

> *I had an aunt who lived in the maid's quarters of my grandparents' house in Maine. She was my father's sister, an intelligent, creative, eccentric woman who never married. Aunt Pearl was sweet, but she terrified me. She seemed so alone. Unmoored. I never wanted to be like that. Facing the world as a single woman seemed like the biggest failure in life. It pains me that I'm looking at doing this now. It connects to all kinds of things in my life, ways I could never stand on my own. The downside of a happy marriage is you get to coast. But if one of you dies, the other's still coasting.*

I suggested to Eve that debunking this story could be the first step to the rest of her life. As she rummaged through the shadow bag, she found related narratives that exacerbated her melancholy: "People feel sorry for single women," "I will never love again," "My mother never really loved me," "Sexually, I'm past my prime and wouldn't take my clothes off in front of a new man." Eve uncovered a whole range of stories she'd unwittingly secreted into her shadow. As a friend, I guided her through this writing process quite intimately and it hastened her return to the land of the living. Five years later, Eve is going to Kathmandu with her Christian care group. She'll be feeding undernourished children and teaching them to read, activities she and her husband dreamed of doing together but never had the chance. To do this, she needed to touch the shadow. Now, it's time to write about your own shadow parts and listen to their stories.

Core Insights

- ☐ In Jungian psychology, the shadow refers to what remains unconscious in us—both negative and positive.

- ☐ We put into the shadow parts of ourselves that are threatening, embarrassing, confusing, vulnerable-making, wounded, or worse, but we must examine the shadow's contents if we are to grow.

- ☐ When we suppress our gifts in the shadow, they often come out in unhealthy ways as we seek to fill the void with destructive semi-pleasures.

- ☐ We must learn to pass through the shadow for self-realization.

Dive Deeper

Here are four questions that can help you reveal and accept the contents of your shadow bag. It's best to write your responses to these shadow questions as quickly as you can, without forethought or censorship.

- What is the source of your greatest shame? How does it affect your life?

- How much of yourself do you keep hidden? Are you secretive or are you an open book? Are you comfortable knowing that you have a shadow?

- Make a list of five people you dislike intensely. Write a profile of each and explain what it is about them that you find so distasteful.

- Write a letter from your Mr. Hyde—also known as your worst self—to your respectable and virtuous self, sharing how much is missed by being so good.

The shadow self, the alter ego, has a voice you must listen to. It's not necessary to do what it says, but its messages and their implications are filled with growth potential. The shadow self walks the threshold between fear and desire—that illuminating edge where we transcend the known and step beyond our shadow, beyond our story, into something new. Fear and desire are deeply connected. The next step on our journey reveals why.

FEAR AND DESIRE

As humans, we are all too aware that desire and fear are two sides of the same stick. Anyone who's ever been madly in love, or devoted to a goal, or enamored of anything at all, knows how closely fear shadows desire. It's hard to have one without the other, it seems (though we will debunk this false claim soon). How can you want love without fearing its loss? Commit yourself fully to a goal without fear of failure? Give yourself wholeheartedly to your own life without worrying that it will end? We've struggled with this conflict since time immemorial, caught between seemingly opposing forces.

What's more, we fear the force of desire itself because it threatens to change the status quo: the story of who we are and who we're not. Desire doesn't care about minding the rules or coloring inside the lines; it's free and anarchic by nature. In Greek mythology, the god of desire, Eros, is shadowed in the world by his sister, Chaos. We're all too aware that when desire is indulged mindlessly it has the potential to destroy what we love. In an effort to protect what we've built, including our identity, we may even deny our desires altogether in deference to our fears. This robs us of vitality and the willingness to tell the truth. Here's a short list of desires that commonly scare us:

Fear of abandoning ourselves to passion

Fear of pursuing unconventional dreams

Fear of losing someone or something we love

Fear of failing at a challenge we care about

Fear of freedom and free will

Fear of power and success

Fear of being our true self

This list could go on and on. We fight off what we most desire in confusing, detrimental ways that often keep us in bondage to fear. This self-sabotage makes no rational sense. Why would anyone be afraid of success or freedom? Yet the shadow beckons us to abandon desires that risk changing our story or altering our self-image. We are likely to keep such desires, which may be sources of shame in themselves, safely out of sight—if we acknowledge them at all.

Beverly was an eighty-year-old spitfire trapped in a claustrophobic marriage. Beverly was a study in opposites: a strong-minded, brilliant, nonconformist who was afraid to stand up to her bossy husband. She'd mastered the art of pretending not to have desires—especially the desire for time alone. "He's like a boa constrictor," she wrote, "sucking the life right out me." I asked Beverly to write about the dynamic of fear and desire in her life. What was stopping her from stating her needs and claiming her autonomy? Here is her response.

> *It's a case of the "the devil you know"—I know what it's like to be strangled; I don't know what it's like to be free. That's the truth. I grew up with an oppressive father and a mother who told me that without a man, a woman is nothing. In those days, that was the story they fed us. I bought that misogynist myth hook, line, and sinker!*

As Beverly continued to explore the truth of her feelings, she realized that fear was tangled up with authentic desires to travel, pursue alternative health care, publish her poetry, and fulfill a lifelong dream by moving to the country. Her marital troubles were mere symptoms of a larger malaise: a habit of self-sabotage that was caused by voices from the shadow she had never explored. As she articulated these voices on paper, Beverly was surprised how quickly their hold on her loosened. Three months after the course ended, she sent me a postcard from Italy, where she'd traveled with friends, without her husband. He had resisted but, to her amazement, had backed down when she threatened to leave him. She wrote: "All those years I thought *he* was stopping me, when in fact, I was stopping myself and using him as a big excuse."

We all use fear as an excuse not to be ourselves or admit to our authentic desires in life. We tell ourselves stories about why we're trapped, fortifying those stories—and the fears they mask—through repetition. Like Beverly, we may constrict ourselves and blame others for our own fears. But the moment we recognize this pattern, it can begin to shift. We can assume responsibility for our own desires, whether or not we choose to pursue them. No longer the victim, we can face our fears and find out what's behind them. Take time to explore the following list of common desires shadowed by fear and see how they play into your own life.

Core Insights

- [ ] We fight off what we most desire in confusing, detrimental ways that often keep us in bondage to fear.

- [ ] The shadow beckons us to abandon desires that risk changing our story or smashing our self-image altogether.

- [ ] We use fear as an excuse not to be ourselves or admit to our authentic desires in life.

- [ ] When we assume responsibility for our own desires, we can face our fears and find out what's behind them.

Dive Deeper

Write about your experience with each of the following fears and desires. Give concrete examples, exploring the stories behind your fears and what might happen if you pursued this desire.

Fear of abandoning yourself to passion

Fear of pursuing unconventional dreams

Fear of losing someone or something we want love

Fear of failing at a challenge we care about

Fear of freedom and free will

Fear of power and success

Fear of being authentic and truthful

When you realize the strength of your desire-and-fear stories, and how they define what you believe is possible, you make way for courageous choices, as well as breakthroughs in self-acceptance. You discover that your shadow can be a refuge, in fact, when you make it your ally.

FINDING YOUR INNER REFUGE

When I went to India for the first time, I traveled to Ladakh, the northernmost province of the country that used to be part of Tibet. Ladakh is a land filled with Buddhist temples and one day, while visiting one these temples, I wandered into a darkened back room where I came upon a "secret Buddha," an unassuming life-sized figure hidden away from public view. Unlike the grand, ostentatious statue at the temple entrance, this secret Buddha had an air of sacredness precisely because it was tucked away inside its own private refuge. The secret Buddha was surrounded by images of demons that symbolized hatred, fear, and greed; yet instead of threatening The Enlightened One, these figures appeared to be protecting him. Having conquered his demons by confronting them, the Buddha had realized his own true nature, turned former enemies into allies, and transmuted negativity into strength.

Similarly, when you face your fears and desires through writing, you transform resistance into courage and gain access to your own inner refuge. It is a sanctuary of self-awareness that becomes your base of operations on this writing journey. No longer frightened of your own shadow, or scared of being alone with yourself, you learn to access this sanctuary at will and renew your courage through self-reflection. Becoming your own secret Buddha, you uncover the gifts of solitude and vision only found in darkness and shadow. "In a dark time, the eye begins to see," wrote the poet Theodore Roethke. Entering the dark, you see through different eyes and surprising insights begin to appear. This can't happen in the glare of exposure and daylight. Just as newborn babies are unable to see in the sunlight, your new eyes need darkness and protection in order to focus. The two greatest challenges in writing practice—solitude and entering the shadow—are also the doorways to self-revelation. You can't see yourself clearly in society's glare, nor write about deepest feelings and thoughts when barraged with outside stimulation.

Solitude is different from loneliness. Solitude is rich, inspiring, and restful; replete with space and possibility. Loneliness is empty, pathetic, and enervating; bereft of power and potential. Lonely people expect others to fill their inner void, whereas lovers of solitude—which is what I invite you to become on this journey— recognize that time alone is precious, a refuge where you can practice meeting yourself in the mirror of the blank page.

Let's do an exercise together. Take out a pen and piece of paper. Imagine yourself in a solitary place, enjoying the silence. Imagine that your body is light and open, receptive to subtle thoughts and feelings. Then write for five minutes without stopping about a challenge you face in your life today.

When time is up, take out another piece of paper. Imagine yourself somewhere stranded and alone, calling out, and no one answers—like a child abandoned in its crib. Feel that desolation and loneliness in your gut. Then write for five minutes without stopping about something that gives you a lot of joy.

As you finish, notice how that exercise went. Was it hard for you to do? Did cognitive dissonance interfere with your ability to write about pain while feeling peaceful or joy while feeling lonely? This exercise shows how the atmosphere of your inner refuge affects your ability to do this writing practice. If your internal atmosphere is tense and threatening, you will have a harder time expressing the truth about your experience, even when it's positive. If the atmosphere is relaxed and protected, you'll have an easier time exploring your thoughts and feelings, including the contents of your shadow. Here are five useful tools for cultivating and protecting your inner refuge:

Practice regularly. Whenever possible, write at the same time each day for at least five consecutive days a week. By devoting time to your practice, you create a reliable space, which helps to invite the subconscious, your muse, to come forward.

Make a nest. It's best to write in the same place, but when it's not possible, make a writing nest. This means having a comfortable place to sit, as much quiet as possible, and visuals that work for you. Some people like an open window nearby, others prefer a Zen-style blank wall.

Leave the outside world outside. It's important to focus, and even the most solitary place can feel hectic if you can't keep the outside world out of your mind. Develop a meditation, yoga, breathing, or prayer practice to help you settle the mind before writing. Five minutes of doing a preparation practice is more than enough.

Emphasize love, not fear. It's important to free writing from pain, self-judgment, or obligation. This means refraining from self-attack when you're doing this practice. No matter what happens, if you're sitting in front of a blank page you've already succeeded. When you remember to show up, anything that happens after that will be good—even if you can't write at all. If that happens, write about not being able to write. That'll get the pen or keyboard moving.

Enjoy your solitude. As writers, we must learn to enjoy our own company. We must enjoy visiting our own minds, hearing what we have to say, and remembering that we are okay on our own. We can step away from the crowd and neither panic nor lose a sense of who we are. Practice enjoying the unfilled space and hearing the sounds within the silence.

Your inner refuge will serve you well once you take the time to make your own. These deepening practices will help you create that sanctuary.

Core Insights

☐ When we face our fears and desires through writing, we gain access to a self-awareness that becomes our base of operations on this writing journey.

☐ By entering the dark, we see through different eyes and surprising insights begin to appear.

☐ The two greatest challenges in writing practice—solitude and entering the shadow—are also the doorways to self-revelation.

☐ Enjoy solitude. As writers, we must be able to enjoy our own company.

Dive Deeper

Set aside an hour for this series of short writing exercises. Take ten minutes to explore each of the following topics. Try not to edit or reread.

• Are you able to create a schedule and stick to it? Is regularity a challenge for you? How does this affect your life and writing?

- Are you someone who knows how to make a nest? Can you create comfort and protection in your life? How does this affect your life and writing?

- Do you have trouble unplugging? Is it hard to say "no" to the outside world? How does this affect your life and writing?

- Are you able to tolerate love without conflict, peace without internal agitation? Many people are unwittingly addicted to tumult, division, and upheaval. For writers, this can make practice a hell realm. Are you someone like this? If so, how does this affect your life and writing? If not, what tools do you use to defuse negative thinking?

- Does being alone make you feel lonely? Is solitude something you value? In your experience, what is the difference between these two states? Give examples. How does your attitude toward being alone affect your life and writing?

As long as you have a strong inner refuge, you can venture deep on this writing journey without losing your balance. You can meet your true face in the mirror and know that there is much more to learn.

3 Your True Face

This chapter is about the origins of personal identity. Beginning with the bond between mother (or primary caregiver) and you as a child, we'll explore how your earliest stories have been formed through attachment, touch, and the transmission of empathy. We'll delve into the myth of the inner child, the nature of innocence, and the wisdom we are born with when we enter this world. Part of that wisdom is *Beginner's Mind*—the ability to meet each moment without prejudice—in writing and in life. This introduces the witness, the objective wisdom mind that enables us to perceive our thoughts and feelings clearly enough to translate them onto the written page.

THE MOTHERING GAZE

We learn the world from the face of our mother or primary caregiver. From the doting reflection of a guardian's eyes, a baby draws its earliest, wordless lessons about connection, care, tenderness, and safety. According to Dan Siegel, a psychologist who specializes in early bonding, every child yearns for this gaze. And they must have it for healthy emotional development to occur. This eye contact determines how we come to view ourselves and the narrative we later create from that view. Why would this mothering gaze be so influential? It all comes down to imitation. "We learn to care, quite literally, by observing the caring behavior of our parents toward us," Siegel explains. Children deprived of the mothering gaze are more likely to feel disconnected from others later in life.

That's why if you hope to understand your story, it's important to inquire into how you were viewed and loved as a child.

Emotional groundwork is laid by the time we are seven months old, so long before you began to speak, an encyclopedia of preverbal information was transmitted to your baby brain. If your caregiver was responsive to your needs and interacted with you in a sensitive way, you're more likely to form a secure attachment that leads to emotional resilience and confidence. If you were deprived of the mothering gaze, you're more likely to develop an insecure attachment that can lead to low self-esteem and a struggle to feel a sense of belonging. Secure children tend to be more empathic and bond more easily with others, while insecure kids can have trouble connecting and accepting intimacy.

These are not hard and fast rules. There are neglected children who as adults work doubly hard to open their hearts, and individuals with doting parents who respond by taking love for granted. The point is that your story of self is deeply rooted in messages you received as a baby. Major themes of that story include your ability to love and be loved, feel as if you belong in the world, know your worth, connect with others, feel safe rather than threatened, and be strong and independent rather than abandoned and needy. All of these have their earliest roots in the primal relationship between you and your first caregiver.

Two of my students had childhood experiences that illustrate this important point. Jesse was the only child in a privileged family whose mother was clinically depressed during much of his early life. Jesse grew up feeling alone in the world, despite wealth and a loving circle of family and friends. His roommate, Natasha, was one of eleven kids in a low-income family, whose mother was nurturing, present, and supportive without being clingy. Their responses to the question, "What did you learn from your mother's face?" were as varied as their childhood experiences.

Jesse: *It's dangerous to ask for love. I'm not a deeply lovable person. There are unforgivable flaws in me, and nothing I do can make up for them. I try and try and the gap gets bigger, like when you reach for something in water and it*

*keeps bouncing away, out of touch. That's how I feel about
intimacy. Every time I try to grab it, it's gone. I can't
connect! This leaves me feeling like a total failure.*

Natasha: *My mother's face told me that I would survive;
that no matter what happened, we were strong. This gave
me a crazy confidence that comes to my rescue when I need
it the most. Even when I'm down and out, I can think of
my mother and I always feel better. If she could do it, I can
do it. If she could love me, and all of us kids, with nobody
around to help her, I can sure be as loving when my life's
not perfect. I learned that just because things aren't going
your way, it doesn't mean there's something wrong with
you. If you hang in there and don't give up, somehow you
will find your way. The bottom line is: I trust myself.*

It wasn't hard to identify the core beliefs in each of these
submissions or how they were linked to the mothering gaze. The
child with the absent mother felt that no matter how deep his
longing, he would remain unsatisfied because of a crucial flaw in
himself. The child with the attentive mother built her identity
around the story that outer events were no match for inner fortitude or the power of togetherness. One story enabled Natasha to
thrive even in the midst of adversity, and the other story shows how
insecure attachment was an ongoing handicap that kept Jesse
unhappy and alienated.

I chose these two examples because they fall squarely into one
camp or the other: secure or insecure attachment. In many of our
lives, these camps overlap, making our memories more mixed and
fluid. The mothers we remember had good days and bad days—
sometimes they were attentive and sometimes absent—and there
were times we felt loved and times when we seemed invisible.

As you focus on this early bond, remember to emphasize emotional memory rather than your story about those emotions. As
you write, notice how your body feels and bring that information

to the page. The body holds emotion and memory as much as the mind does. Visceral experience tends to be more dependable than concepts, ideas, or rationales. These questions will help you explore all of this.

Core Insights

☐ Every child must experience eye contact from a primary caregiver in order for healthy emotional development to occur.

☐ If we're deprived of the mothering gaze, we're more likely to develop an insecure attachment that can lead to low self-esteem and a struggle to feel a sense of belonging.

☐ Secure children tend to be more empathic and to bond more easily with others, while insecure kids often have trouble connecting and being comfortable with intimacy.

☐ The body holds emotion and memory as much as the mind does, and visceral experience tends to be more dependable than concepts, ideas, and rationales.

Dive Deeper

• What did you learn from the face of your mother or primary caregiver? What did this face tell you about yourself and the world?

• How were you loved as a child or how were you not loved? What did this experience teach you about your own ability to love? How has this pattern manifested in your relationships?

- Are you secure in your attachments to others? Or do you experience insecure attachment? How does this affect your ability to bond?

- Does trust come easily to you, or are you prone to self-defense? Do you view others as enemies or soon-to-be traitors, or do you give others the benefit of the doubt?

Once you've started to pull back the layers of emotion and memory derived from this earliest of bonds, you realize that within your grown-up self lives a child who will never grow up—and shouldn't. This child has its own wisdom to share as you continue on this writing journey.

THE WISE CHILD

Many of us have difficulty remembering ourselves before the age of five. There may be flashes, images, and half-recollections of intense or traumatizing moments. But few of us can recall how it felt to be a child from day to day. You've probably heard stories about things your child-self did, seen photographs of yourself as a baby and toddler, and been told details about scenes you lived through. But second-hand tales are just that: other people's memories. While you contained the ingredients of the person you were to become, as an acorn prefigures the oak tree, you hadn't yet formed an identity capable of making its own choices for its own reasons, mindful of its own consequences.

At the same time, the child-self has wisdom. The child-self is awake in ways the adult-self is not, even without worldly knowledge or experience. Innocence has its own kind of wisdom that dims with time as identity weaves its limiting story and turns us away from our source. For millennia, philosophers, poets, and psychologists have sung the praises of the Wise Child, or the Divine Child. They point to the child-self's overlooked gifts and its secret link to the life of the spirit. "Genius is nothing more nor less than childhood recovered at will," wrote the poet Charles Baudelaire. What exactly does the Wise Child know, and how can we reclaim its innocence?

Stella was a would-be novelist who came to me for help with her book. She'd been blocked in her writing for some time, unable to complete her first novel, a story about a girl magician with supernatural powers. Having drafted the first half, Stella hit a roadblock when her heroine has to battle an evil character who's taken her magic away. Stella had already tried many approaches to overcoming writer's block, and came to me hoping to uncover the psychological cause for her artistic troubles. I asked Stella to begin by doing a brief character sketch of the protagonist and antagonist in her book.

> Protagonist: *X is an orphan. Innocent. Spunky. Parents are trapped in an underground prison. Disobeyed order to kill her at birth. Needs magic to save them. Y stole her powers. X can't live without them.*

> Antagonist: *Y is afraid of X's magic. He wants it for himself. Feeds on her fear. Y is a coward. No heart. Lives in the shadows. A fallen angel. Starving. But for what?*

It seemed possible that X and Y were stand-ins for two sides of Stella's own psyche. She protested this idea as simplistic, yet the more we explored these two characters, the more Stella's true feelings began to surface. She felt closer to Y than to X, the villain was misunderstood, the imprisoned parents were evil themselves, and the heroine X was an impostor—brainwashed to believe her magic was good, when in fact it had caused all this trouble. With this confusion, it wasn't surprising that Stella was blocked in her story. Her characters' motives were so mixed up.

As we worked together, Stella's story emerged. As a child, she had been sexually abused by a favorite uncle. When she told her parents, they pressed charges, and the uncle was arrested. Stella spent a miserable childhood blaming herself, resenting her parents, and wishing she'd never told them what happened. Her parents remained judgmental of Stella's choices, attributed her failures to this early trauma, and treated her like damaged goods. The novel was Stella's attempt to create a new story to reclaim her innocence or magic, battle with forces of evil, and forgive herself for everything.

I encouraged Stella to explore her true feelings about what happened and the emotional paralysis it caused. She eventually came to see how turned-around her story had been. It wasn't Stella's magic, or innocence, that had caused her to be molested; nor had this magic been robbed from her. Her child-self remained intact beneath this layer of adaptive fiction. Once she saw that, no battle to wrest good from evil was necessary. Stella didn't need it to put her life right, since she was not damaged goods. By listening to the voice of the Wise Child still living within her, Stella saw that she didn't need to invent monsters in a fantasy world, she just needed to stop the monsters in her head from running her life. She set out to write a memoir instead.

What does the Wise Child inside you know that the grown-up may have forgotten? These deepening practices will help you find out.

Core Insights

- ☐ The child-self is awake in ways the adult-self is not, even without worldly knowledge or experience.

- ☐ We embody a natural wisdom as children that dims with time as identity weaves its story of limiting beliefs and disconnection from our source.

- ☐ As Charles Baudelaire wrote, "Genius is nothing more or less than childhood recovered at will."

☐ Children come into the world bearing gifts of great importance and beauty, but we generally overlook these gifts.

Dive Deeper

- Do you remember feeling innocent or guilty as a child? How did this story begin in you?

- What did you know as a child that you would like to learn again or remember? How would this benefit your life?

- Do you resist the childlike parts of yourself? If so, why? Be specific.

- Write a monologue in the child's voice, describing a current life conflict that requires resolution. What advice would your child-self give you?

Acknowledging the child's voice of wisdom gives you access to the genius you were born with. For now, it's enough to know that this awakened, childlike perspective is still within you. In the next lesson, we'll look at a practice that offers a gateway to that perspective.

BEGINNER'S MIND

Children are born with Beginner's Mind. The world appears new, free of labels and concepts. Before story begins to obscure things, a child lives in direct contact with her surroundings. This ability to see things as they are, directly, is the essence of the awakened state. It is also the state we cultivate in our writing practice. The concept of Beginner's Mind is rooted in Zen Buddhism; it is an open mind that can see things as they are. "If your mind is empty, it is always ready for anything, it is open to everything," wrote Shunryū Suzuki. "In the beginner's mind there are many possibilities, but in the expert's mind there are few." That's why all spiritual practice, including writing to awaken, aims to see reality as it is by unlearning what we think we know and telling the truth without interpretation.

In our intellectual culture, value is placed on how much we know. We're brainwashed into believing that being a beginner is a stage to grow out of as quickly as possible in order to become a master of the universe. We're taught that the smartest person wins and that smartness comes from gathering, memorizing, and storing the greatest amount of information. This prepares us to be knowledgeable, to master the outside world, to expertly recite facts and figures—without necessarily knowing ourselves. We pay little attention to what's inside of us, our inner life, our moment-to-moment existence. This is why intellectually brilliant people can also be emotionally ignorant and devoid of self-knowledge. We can be so busy thinking and doing that we forget how to simply be.

Every creative person knows that invention, imagination, and creativity happen when we let go of what we know and allow ourselves to be guided. Creativity comes from not knowing, from surrender and discovery—not from thinking. The thinking mind is good for many things, but most that truly matter—like love, art, faith, friendship, passion, and joy—do not arise from the intellect. Instead, they arise from a mind that is open, inquisitive, flexible, and child-like. They come from Beginner's Mind. When you ask yourself direct questions, answer them truthfully, then respond to what you've written, you are cultivating this direct way of seeing. To be truthful, you must be present—so if you're not paying attention, the truth will elude you. As you write, you may realize how distracted you are, with a mind that heads in a hundred directions.

Try this exercise. Wherever you are right now, bring stillness to your inner refuge. Once you've done this, look around very slowly, carefully, and intensely. Become aware of yourself in space and of the many things around and within you. Just be here in this very moment. With this present awareness, respond to the question, "Who am I here and now?" Take twelve minutes to write about how you see yourself in this very moment, using Beginner's Mind. Here's an example.

> *I'm at my white desk, late morning, crystal Buddha, no sun, chicken salad on a pita, green plate, cracked coffee cup, oleander plant blowing, cold wind outside. Feeling creaky, shouldn't sit hunched like this at the keyboard. Ideas coming fast, but my foot is shaking and that's annoying. What does that tell me about my stress?*

If you follow your attention with language, it will create a 3-D representation of the present moment, including the landscape of your inner world. This is a good exercise for learning to see yourself with Beginner's Mind and to then write with that sensitivity. The more you do this, the more it becomes second nature. Start from where you are. Try these deepening practices to help you develop a fresh perspective.

Core Insights

☐ Children are born with Beginner's Mind and the ability to see things as they are. Spiritual practice helps us see reality as it is and tell the truth without interpretation.

☐ In our intellectual culture, we're taught that knowledge comes from gathering, memorizing, and storing the greatest amount of information.

☐ Creativity comes from not knowing. Love, faith, friendship, passion, and joy arise from a mind that is open, inquisitive, flexible, and child-like.

☐ By asking ourselves direct questions and answering them truthfully, we cultivate this direct way of seeing and become more present in our lives.

Dive Deeper

- Describe yourself and your surroundings at this moment. Include inner and outer experiences and what you perceive with your senses. Be as detailed and thorough as possible.

- Write about your relationship with routine. Are you rigidly attached to your habits? If so, which ones, and why? How does attachment to routine limit your ability to be spontaneous?

- Take a short walk in your neighborhood and try to remember everything you see and hear. Then write about what you remember. The next day, take the same walk and notice what you hadn't seen or heard the day before. Then write about what you forgot or over-looked.

When you open to Beginner's Mind, you will realize how much of your life is happening unnoticed. Trapped in your stories, you are absent from the present moment, living in an open-eyed trance. As you cultivate Beginner's Mind, and the Witness consciousness it awakens, this begins to change.

THE WITNESS

Writing relies on a type of consciousness that offers an objective lens for observation. This Witness consciousness is known in psychology as "metacognition," the uniquely human ability to observe ourselves in the act of thinking. This self-reflecting capacity enables us to know ourselves in ways that other animals can't: from the outside-in. We can see how we label our own experience and then turn those labels into stories—all through language.

The Witness is the storyteller and also the inner eye that sees beyond the story. Using Beginner's Mind, we can cultivate the Witness and learn to step out of the flood of experience onto the banks of our mental river. From there, we can watch experience passing by. This is not disassociation because, when we write from the Witness perspective, we're fully embodied, alert, and connected. Rather than deny our experience, we embrace it all—even painful experiences—and include what we are seeing, feeling, and thinking. By stepping onto the banks of awareness, we create a half-inch of distance between the story and the part of consciousness that is watching the flow. This is how transformation happens, because we are acknowledging a part of us that is always and forever free.

The Witness is not an identity, nor a separate self that lurks inside the mind or body. It is neither subject nor object. Instead, it's the omnipresent beingness that operates within all of us. As mental chatter calms and inner clarity increases during meditation and contemplative practice, we are able to meet this Witness. It feels like a long-lost friend who knows us better than we know ourselves. When you engage the Witness while writing, it helps quiet the brilliant, inventive left hemisphere of the brain. The discursive mind settles, and your intuition and emotional intelligence can emerge.

Russell was a guy who couldn't sit still. Kinetic, ambitious, and obsessed with goals, Russell was a take-charge person who tended toward linear, black-and-white thinking. This helped him succeed in business, but blocked him in his personal life because reality is not a spreadsheet and happiness can't be put on a graph. Women adored Russell at first, and then fled from him because after his initial charm wore off, they discovered a rigid, inattentive man who didn't express feelings or pick up on their emotional signals. In his first assignment for our course, he was clear about his intention.

I'm here because a woman I'm crazy about is going to leave me if things don't change. She says I need to "drop in," whatever that means. She says I'm just "not there." I lack "self-awareness." I think she's confusing self-awareness with navel-gazing, to tell you the truth. But since I hate psychotherapy, can't meditate, and have no interest in self-help in general, I figure I might as well try writing.

I asked Russell to read over what he submitted and write about his own impressions, to see more deeply into his words, objectively, in search of the truth. If he observed his writing without preconceptions, as if it had been done by someone else, what did Russell see? His response contained both surprise and annoyance.

The guy sounds pretty self-absorbed. He doesn't seem to be listening to the woman, just doing what he must do to keep her happy, or less unhappy, so she won't leave him. His use of quotes seems sarcastic, like he's defending himself. The whole thing reads kind of arrogantly. He shoots down what she believes in (therapy, meditation, yoga) because he's jealous. It's obvious! I never saw it that way before.

Russell offers an extreme example of a very common condition. When we're inside the story, we overlook the Witness. As he examined his own writing, he stepped outside his experience for the first time and encountered "the shock of the real" as Russell saw how he appeared from the outside. He observed and, more importantly, felt his psyche as it was reflected on the page. This mirror allowed him to see what his girlfriend complained about. This led him to reveal a secret fear in his next submission.

My father always told me it's bad luck to second-guess yourself, because "he who hesitates is lost." So I turned into someone who never stopped to look in the mirror in any deep way, fearing what I might see if I did. If I kept running around the bases, I could score without taking a time-out. Just do the next thing, make the next sale, solve the next problem. You can't "be there" if you're always running. I think I've been running my whole life.

As Russell reread his own writing week after week, he became more familiar with self-reflection. The Witness could see what Russell, caught up in nonstop activity, could not. Writing forced him to slow down and allowed his mind and heart to open. It also showed Russell what he'd been missing by running away from his reflection: "If I can't look at myself," he wrote, "how can I expect to see anyone else?" This life-changing insight helped heal his relationships with his girlfriend and himself.

Your Witness is your greatest ally, both in writing and in life. As you move into the next section, remember that the Witness is there to help you see clearly. Using its clear lens, you can separate the wheat of truth from the chaff of self-deception. This will be enormously helpful as you come to explore your personal story with the blinders taken off.

Core Insights

☐ The Witness consciousness is the uniquely human ability to observe ourselves in the act of thinking.

☐ The Witness is the storyteller and the inner eye that sees beyond the story.

☐ As mental chatter calms down and inner clarity increases during meditation and contemplative practice, we are able to meet the Witness.

☐ When we engage the Witness while writing, it helps quiet the left hemisphere of the brain, and intuition and emotional intelligence can emerge.

Dive Deeper

- What does the Witness know, right now, that you would be wise to acknowledge? Looking at your life from the outside, what do you need to see? Why does this recognition matter?

- How does hyperactivity or an inability to concentrate block you from self-reflection? What can the Witness show you about what you're missing? What steps can you take to slow down?

- When and why do you disassociate in life? Give examples of when you tend to check out or cut yourself off from feelings. What effect does disassociation have on your experience? The ability to form intimate connections? The satisfaction of savoring experience?

- After you've responded to these prompts, put your writing aside for at least one day. Then reread your responses to questions 1, 2, and 3. Comment on what you see without judgment or prejudice, one piece of writing at a time.

When you strengthen the Witness, you can step outside your story and observe mental activity from an objective distance. As your greatest ally on this writing journey, the Witness opens the door to a new level of self-understanding. We'll use this perspective to move into the next phase of discovery: exploring the story of who you are.

Part Two

EXPLORING THE STORY

4 Demons at the Gate

There are four crucial adversaries on the path of self-discovery that we must confront using the Witness consciousness. If we don't face these demons, we are unable to explore our story objectively or write truthfully about what we find.

Resistance is the ego's first line of defense against exposing its cherished myths. Next, it unleashes the twin demons of narcissism and self-doubt, with their cynical strategies for sabotaging insight. This leads to another destructive duo, guilt and shame, that block the vulnerability of full disclosure. Then there's fear of humiliation, a universal aversion that can trick the mind into sticking harder to the story. Confronting these demons one by one, you will see that when you look them in the eye they quickly lose their power—and that doing so frees you to tell the whole truth.

RESISTANCE

As you've noticed, writing sometimes evokes resistance. Moving toward the light of awareness calls our demons to rise from the shadows and block the way. Our ego does not want to give up its stories or question its sovereignty. This back and forth between progress and resistance is a natural part of the growth process that unfolds within writing and other pursuits.

Resistance serves an important purpose on the path of awakening. It tests your mettle and commitment, and strengthens you for the journey ahead. It's one thing to have a moment of insight; it's quite another thing to claim the insight and stand up to forces that aim to destroy it. Like adventurers on any quest for treasure, we must face the demons that guard the gate of self-knowledge and block access to the truth we're seeking. We confront these demons head on, expose their weaknesses, and slay them. In this conflict, questions are your weapons and self-inquiry is the battle plan.

While resistance to change takes many forms, all share a common source: fear. Whether fear manifests as shame, disgust, antipathy, aggression, disinterest, judgment, or any of a thousand other responses, it serves the same purpose: to protect the self-serving stories that maintain sovereignty of the ego and its status quo. To understand this counterproductive process, it's helpful to understand how the personal ego works.

The word "ego" comes from the Latin word for "I." At its most basic level, ego is the mental formation of "I" that arises in children in response to a fear of not existing. Having noticed that they're separate from the mother, children realize they're not omnipotent and begin to create their identity in the form of protest. In the stage known as the "terrible twos," toddlers try to establish a foothold in a world they can't control by resisting whatever comes their way with a single, reflexive response: "No!" Each time a child says no, the belief in himself and his personal boundary solidifies. Over time, these negating boundaries delineate the child's sense of self, form its identity, and create the story of who he is by protesting loudly against who he's not. Ego is an accumulation of many "No!" moments and survives primarily through resistance.

That's why anything that threatens our sense of self—including positive information—is viewed as an enemy by our ego. It's the reason we sometimes resist change for the good. Fatima learned this when attempting to dismantle her own tragic story. A refugee from a war-torn country, Fatima came to my course hoping to heal. She'd witnessed unimaginable horrors, including the murders of family members, and longed to neutralize these nightmare memories through writing. "I don't want to be defined by tragedy," Fatima wrote in her first submission. "I want to be free—to begin a new story. That's all I want now. Liberation." Fatima threw herself into her writing as if trying to save her own life. She allowed herself to describe previously unspeakable events and their emotional fallout, recalling goon squads, public executions, and the loss of her family home. She expressed relief to finally be writing about things so long hidden, and began to imagine a happier future. For several weeks, this progress continued. Then, suddenly, she dropped out of class.

Concerned, I wrote to Fatima. Had writing triggered past trauma, perhaps? Had something gone wrong in her personal life? Her response was not what I expected. Far from prompting a negative reaction, Fatima assured me the weeks of writing had been a salvation. She felt lighter and happier in her own skin than she had in all the years since the war ended. Nonetheless, Fatima found herself unable to continue.

> *I sat down to write, but nothing happened. I felt guilty for sharing these terrible things, like I was betraying the ghosts of my family. Why should I deserve to be happy? How could I leave them to suffer alone? Their story is my story too. I can't just leave them behind. This is my penance. It's who I am.*

Fatima had realized she wasn't the tragic narrative she'd used to define herself. But this good news appeared as a threat, a stop sign, a warning of danger ahead. Self-defeating as this response was, she couldn't surmount the dread she felt over leaving the past behind in order to wake up to new possibilities—including the threat of being happy. It took years for Fatima to face this resistance, to see it for the demon it was, and return to writing about the war. As she came to understand that guilt and shame were her enemies, along with a fear of self-reinvention, she began writing a memoir that she hopes to publish in her native country.

Whatever the nature of your resistance, you can be sure it's a sign of progress. When you're writing, discomfort will often arise in proportion to how much of the truth you are willing to tell.

When this happens, the best thing to do is keep going. Acknowledge the demons of fear and foreboding, and ask them to kindly move out of the way. You may be amazed by how acquiescent they are. And if they continue their stand, you can keep writing through them anyway. In the end, you will befriend these demons for making you stronger and keeping you honest. These deepening prompts will help you make their acquaintance and not be fooled by their fierce appearances.

Core Insights

☐ The back and forth between progress and resistance is a natural part of the growth process in writing and other pursuits.

☐ Resistance to change takes many forms, all with a common source of fear. It serves an important purpose on the path of awakening, as it tests your mettle and commitment, and strengthens you for the journey ahead.

☐ The word "ego" comes from the Latin word for "I." It is the mental formation that arises in response to the fear of not existing. Each time a child says "No!" he solidifies boundaries. Ego is an accumulation of many "No!" moments and survives primarily through resistance.

☐ When we're writing, discomfort will often arise in proportion to how much of the truth we are willing to tell.

Dive Deeper

• Describe three demons that have already appeared on your path as forms of resistance that threatened to stop you. Once you've done this, write a demon monologue for each resistance, using the voice of that saboteur. See what it is trying to tell you. Set it aside for at least one day, then reread these demon monologues and respond to their messages using the perspective of the Witness. What does the eye of wisdom see in each of these negative messages? What response will neutralize the destructive power?

- Explore the positive side of resistance, identifying what you've learned from past trials that made you stronger or kept you honest.

- Describe an instance when you fought off positive change, even if you did not mean to. Did you defend a painful situation, rather than surrender to healing? What story did you use to defend your resistance? How did this resistance shift? If it didn't shift, describe why not.

By understanding how resistance works through the tendency to fight off change—even when it's for your own good—you disempower the demons that want to keep you trapped as you are: a "little me" that's bound by a fear of stepping beyond obsolete stories.

NARCISSISM

Among the powerful narratives that keep us stuck is the myth of Narcissus. Like the self-absorbed character in Greek mythology, we move through our lives locked inside our own reflection, seeing the world through a mirrored veil. To create a life from stories is to be a narcissist. While we're all narcissistic to some extent, becoming obsessed with a reflecting pool is an obvious obstacle to writing with clear eyes.

Colm was a handsome Irishman who wanted to write a memoir about finding his biological mother after being raised by adoptive parents. Colm was convinced that it would make a great story. It didn't. With every batch of pages he delivered, my heart sank at the dishonesty of the writing. He was describing a character: not a human being and certainly not himself. He couldn't see past this character's reflection to connect with who he actually was. I told Colm what I thought, but he didn't seem to understand. I used words like "inauthentic," "generic," "lacking emotion," and they flew past his towering, ginger head like so much confetti. Still, he wanted to try.

I asked him to write about his greatest shame. Colm claimed not to have any shame and he delivered a self-inflating sermon on coming out as gay, loud and proud. I asked him if this was true: not one source of shame? Finally, a glimmer of light came with this passage.

> *When I left my Mom to find my real mother, I saw the pain*
> *in her face. I felt ashamed and selfish. She sacrificed a lot*
> *for me. I loved her and now I don't know where I belong.*
> *Like I'm floating and no can really see me.*

As breakthroughs go, Colm had hit pay dirt. He continued to write about not belonging, and revealed a layer of pain and rejection. He'd grown up as the adopted gay son of nice, but backward, religious parents. He was loved but never felt he belonged. His father didn't talk much and never showed emotions; his mother was timid, caring, and weak. Colm felt too big for his surroundings, which prompted him to put up a screen between himself and the rest of the world. He knew it was there, but couldn't remove it. By writing that, of course, Colm had already started to take down the screen and was able to see himself for the first time. He could feel his shame, alienation, and pain—which he'd numbed with bonhomie until he didn't even know they were there.

As a demon in the writing process, narcissism throws us off track when we come close to revealing too much. Narcissists both crave and dread attention; that's what makes them such difficult company. Both craving and dreading attention interfere with writing unselfconsciously. You can't tell the truth if you have one eye on the mirror, asking "How am I doing?" to make sure your reflection holds. Instead, this practice enables us to say "Get out of the way."

Narcissism comes in two basic flavors. A negative narcissist will let everyone know what a loser he is: worthless, broken, and beyond help. He'll suck the air out of a room with chronic, self-directed abnegation and belittlement. A positive narcissist will be a braggart and show off. She is so full of herself that others will virtually disappear in the glow of her superior being. If you want to know which kind of narcissist you are, ask yourself whether you are more likely to praise or blame yourself. If you're being honest, you'll know the answer. Here are two examples of student work that reflect very different self-images.

> Positive Narcissist: *If other people did what I told them to, the world would be a better place. I mean that very honestly. I'm a leader, a winner, and always have been. People don't try hard enough in their lives. They want to ride your coattails. I don't mean that in an unkind way, but there aren't a lot of people to look up to.*

> Negative Narcissist: *I'm totally stuck in my life, I can't move forward. Everything I do turns to crap. It's because of my family, the way they hold me down, like if I were to ever actually be myself it would kill them. If I told the truth it would destroy their lives. Because there's something wrong with me. I'm a gigantic loser.*

Narcissistic writing always circles back to itself. Both types of narcissists repeat themselves, as if yodeling into an echo chamber. They create and repeat the same larger-than-life stories again and again, while blocking out new information. Though most of us don't suffer from this as a personality disorder, we do share elements of this narrative tendency. We create larger-than-life myths about our human-sized selves, and block any information that contradicts these myths.

As you respond to these prompts, notice how you exaggerate positive and negative characteristics, and how you are trapped inside repetitious, self-enclosing stories that block you from being truthful. Also, notice how you write about others. Do you see, hear, and feel the people around you with clarity, or do you perceive others as part of your own reflection? These questions will help you gauge the level of your personal narcissism and how it may interfere with a truthful writing practice.

Core Insights

- ☐ As a demon in the writing process, narcissism throws us off track when we come close to revealing too much.

- ☐ You can't tell the truth if you have one eye on the mirror, asking "How am I doing?" to make sure your reflection holds. Instead, say "Get out of the way."

- ☐ Though most of us do not suffer from narcissism as a personality disorder, we do create larger-than-life myths about our ordinary selves, and block any information that contradicts these myths.

Dive Deeper

- • Write about a cartoon version of yourself that exaggerates your outer qualities and ignores the inner. Describe how this caricature appears to others and the impression it is likely to make on others. Use the third person.

- Do you lean toward positive or negative narcissism? Do you exaggerate your winning or losing qualities? Is your self-talk dominated by praise or blame? Are you grandiose or self-deprecating? How does this tendency influence your choices and self-understanding?

- Describe an experience when you were too self-absorbed, preoccupied, or biased to feel empathy toward a person who needed it. How did you miss the cues? What did you not see or hear? How did you project your own feelings or beliefs onto the other person?

- What sort of attention do you crave from the outside world? What do you want others to appreciate about you? What qualities do you exaggerate to make certain impressions? Why do these impressions matter so much to you?

As you acknowledge narcissistic tendencies and how they affect your ability to see clearly—in writing and in life—you can learn to counter them with mindfulness, humility, and humor. You can admit to what your self-mythologizing exaggerates and what it leaves out. You can recognize how you project this reflection onto the outside world. This will help you neutralize narcissism and see the real roles guilt and shame play in your self-reflecting fantasies.

GUILT AND SHAME

Writing helps us wipe away debris and distortion from our looking glass. What we find underneath the narcissistic cover-up is a layer of self-judgment composed largely of guilt and shame. These twin demons can block us on the writing journey, unless we recognize their destructive power.

Though guilt and shame may seem synonymous, they each carry a different charge and burden us in different ways. Guilt is a moral emotion connected to something we've done or imagine we've done. Shame is an amoral emotion linked with what we believe we are. For example, we might feel guilt for stealing something but shame for being a thief (the label carries social stigma). Though guilt is hardly a pleasant emotion, it can serve a positive social function. It's appropriate to feel guilt when we do something wrong like stealing. Guilt—within reason—can strengthen conscience, protect society, and help us live a moral life. Shame is more insidious than guilt and rarely leads to positive change. As researcher Brené Brown describes it, "shame is an intensely painful feeling or experience of believing that we are flawed and therefore unworthy of love and belonging." Shame has a damning quality that builds on itself and becomes part of our identity.

By exploring your personal story, you'll find that guilt and shame obstruct the truth in distinct ways. Let's say you feel guilty for some lapse in judgment, perhaps an infidelity, and that incident is central to your narrative and self-image. It caused you pain and regret, but you avoided examining the infidelity and its effects on your life, leaving a ripe fruit of insight, waiting to be picked. When you investigate in writing, your guilt may open up other stories and questions in your life concerning unmet needs, emotional commitment, and secret desires. You might discover a longstanding pattern of trespassing healthy boundaries, lying to protect others, or sabotaging intimacy for reasons you don't quite understand. This is how the exploration of a guilt-producing experience can open you up in useful ways by making connections that eluded you before. And these connections might help you stop behaving in ways that hurt yourself and those you love.

Shame is a much harder nut to crack. Let's say this same infidelity has led you to believe you're a fundamentally bad person. The act then becomes secondary to this overarching damnation.

Blinded by shame, it's harder to locate the path to insight because by believing you're rotten to the core, there's little motivation for self-improvement. Shame can preclude positive, lasting change, and can paralyze any desire to write and heal. But where shame may seem impenetrable, emotions are not. A potent way through shame is to question the emotions that shame is hiding, whether it is heartbreak, sadness, helplessness, grief, futility, or loneliness. By looking into these destructive emotions, you can tease out the stories behind them and dissolve the blanketing sense of shame. What you'll find is a generalized unworthiness stemming from early childhood messages of familial, religious, or cultural shaming that accused you of being unworthy simply by being yourself.

When we become aware of our own unworthiness story, it opens the door to a quality whose value we tend to overlook: vulnerability. Without the ability to be vulnerable, it's impossible to write in a truthful way. As in all spiritual practices, the willingness to be vulnerable is a prerequisite to awakening. By dropping pretenses and exposing our shame, we experience a new kind of freedom. We learn that vulnerability leads to authentic strength. These deepening prompts will help you explore how guilt and shame operate in your life, and how increased vulnerability can lead to empowerment.

Core Insights

- ☐ Guilt is a moral emotion connected to something that we have done, whereas shame is an amoral emotion linked with what we believe we are.

- ☐ Guilt can strengthen conscience, protect society, and help us live a moral life. Shame rarely leads to positive change and has a damning quality that becomes part of our identity.

☐ Investigating our guilt through writing may open up questions concerning unmet needs, emotional commitment, and secret desires. Shame may preclude positive, lasting change, and can paralyze the desire to write and heal.

☐ When we become aware of our unworthiness story, we open the door to a vulnerability that allows us to write truthfully and find strength.

Dive Deeper

- Name three actions that make you feel guilty. What part of this guilt is legitimate? How can you make amends for wrongs that you committed or help that you avoided giving?

- What is the source of your greatest shame? When did you first feel ashamed of yourself? Did messages from family, religion, or culture lead to this self-shaming?

- In what areas of your life are you bothered by feelings of unworthiness? Financially? At work? Within love relationships? Tell your unworthiness stories.

- How do you stumble over the threat of vulnerability in your life? How do you shield yourself from exposure? Describe a moment when vulnerability led to a benefit of some kind.

Shame is a formidable demon to confront on this journey, but the vulnerability we are left with is a path to great strength. Having exposed the adversaries of shame and guilt, you can now recognize how they've informed your story. They share a common denominator: humiliation, which is a demon with its own narrative. Let's look at how fear of humiliation locks us into identity.

HUMILIATION

Ambivalence toward vulnerability stems from our fear of humiliation, which lies at the heart of who we are as social creatures. As individuals who depend upon others for our survival, we are hardwired to avoid the rejection that may make us outcasts, scapegoats, or martyrs. Our desire to be inside what sociologists call "the magic circle" of group approval often causes us to compromise our authenticity.

Our fear of self-exposure is deeply connected to the terror of rejection and humiliation. If we risk telling the truth or we dare to question the status quo, we may be exiled from the group—while also losing your own self-respect, stripped of protective narrative. It can be humiliating to realize that the story we've been telling our whole life is little more than a web of make-believe. Nothing is more vulnerable-making than seeing how insecure and uncertain we actually are underneath a puffed-up exterior.

Liam was a college professor who contacted me for a consultation. During our initial call, Liam explained that he'd recently left academia and was toying with the idea of writing a memoir. When I asked him to outline his story, Liam's response was vague and unsatisfying. "I'd say it's the story of a guy *nel mezzo del cammin*—on the threshold of middle age—who's trying to figure out what to do next. He's disenchanted and full of dread. The people in his life have written him off." I told Liam that this sounded more like a diagnosis than a plot. Why was his character disenchanted? What were the causes of his dread? And when had he been "written off" by those around him? This was Liam's response.

> *Those questions seem mostly irrelevant. I don't care about*
> *writing a tell-all book. The literature I like is more*
> *universal. Like the* Divine Comedy. *Dante didn't write*
> *about his childhood pain. Or go into detail about his*
> *biography. He was touching on eternal issues through an*
> *impersonal lens. I want to expose the raw nerve of the*

*human condition without being confessional. But something
is stopping me.*

Liam's resistance to self-exposure suggested that he was not
being honest. There seemed to be a missing link. Even if Liam
chose not to share personal details in the book, it would be helpful
for me, as his mentor, to know what was driving his narrative.
What was the *why* inside the story? What were the stakes for him
as a writer? Two months went by with no response and I assumed
that was the last of Liam. Finally, a three-page email arrived in
which Liam revealed his hidden story.

> *I have a problem with women my own age. I can never
> give them what they want (wedding, mortgage, kids—
> forget it!). That's how I got into trouble with Pam, a
> sophomore in my Italian comp class. Pam and I started
> hanging out during office hours. I could tell she was crazy
> about me. One thing kind of led to another. We met for
> coffee off-campus one afternoon and that's when I made
> a stupid mistake. Basically, I let Pam seduce me. It wasn't
> her fault, I let it happen! She swore not to tell anybody but
> her parents figured it out somehow. I lost my job and got
> raked over the coals in the local paper. Pam never spoke
> to me again, of course. Now I'm forty-one, unemployed,
> and registered as a sexual offender. That's why I need to
> write about this.*

Putting my personal judgment aside, I asked Liam to revisit his
book description. This time, his response came quickly and packed
an emotional punch.

> *It's about crossing from the light into darkness, and
> finding the way to the light again. It's about forbidden
> love, fear of death, betrayal, heartache, and resurrection.
> Also scapegoating and humiliation, which my character*

knows something about! I want to fictionalize the story so that I can really wrestle with these big issues. Just admitting all of this on paper has helped me realize how shut down I've been. The book is about shame and pride as well, and how we betray our own best interests.

I reminded Liam of the literary chestnut "fiction is the lie that tells the truth" and encouraged him to write his novel. Having confronted his humiliation, Liam could fictionalize all he wanted and still the novel would ring true. He finished a first draft of the book, which he plans to publish under a pseudonym with a title torn from the pages of Dante. Having stared down his own demons, Liam managed to come out on top with his writer's voice strong and intact.

Pride is a primary strategy for protecting ourselves from perceived humiliation, but protective pride is a mask to be shed, as Liam found out when he sat down to write. Pride itself is not a bad thing. To be proud of your achievements, your kids, your integrity, is natural and good. But when pride is a defense against humiliation, a cover-up for your imagined weaknesses, failures, and inadequacies, it becomes another demon. Pride can be a form of self-deception. But the small, still voice within will tell you that you're not being honest. This can lead to humility.

Humility, unlike humiliation, is liberating. When you feel humble, you don't mind acknowledging your flaws and getting creative with your limitations. Narcissists resist humility, confusing it with humiliation. They don't care to acknowledge their limitations. The word "humility" comes from the root term for "earth," and grounds us in reality. Where pride closes the heart and defends us from others, humility opens the heart and allows others in. Humility opens the door to wisdom and makes spiritual growth possible, reminding you that the magic circle is within—and that the only person who can put you into exile is yourself.

Core Insights

- [ ] Our ambivalence toward vulnerability stems directly from the fear of humiliation and the desire for group approval.

- [ ] Nothing is more vulnerable-making than seeing how insecure and uncertain we actually are underneath a puffed-up exterior.

- [ ] Pride is a primary strategy for protecting ourselves from perceived humiliation. As a cover-up for our imagined weaknesses, it becomes a demon.

- [ ] Where pride closes the heart and defends us from others, humility opens the heart and allows others in. Humility, unlike humiliation, is liberating.

Dive Deeper

Here are some key questions to write about to help identify, and dissolve, your own fear of humiliation when exploring your personal story.

- How do you respond to the threat of exclusion from your chosen group or from the community into which you were born? Are you willing to tell the truth if it costs you membership in "the magic circle"? Where in your life are you inauthentic in order to gain acceptance and social protection?

- Write about a life experience when negative pride prevented you from being honest. How does negative pride obstruct your ability to be transparent with others? Describe your responses and behaviors as objectively as possible.

- In what areas of your life do you feel "out of tune"? How does this disharmony between your inner and outer lives affect you, or throw you off balance in decision-making and relationships?

- Write about an experience in which you suffered severe humiliation. What was revealed that caused you shame? How could humility have eased this discomfort? Do you associate humility with humiliation? Explore this dichotomy in your life.

Your responses to these questions will help reveal where the lack of humility may be blocking your psychological and spiritual growth, and where pride may be stopping you from self-inquiry. You will learn that the biggest fear of all is that, if you know too much, you will lose respect for, and faith in, your own life myth.

5 The Question of Meaning

As you investigate the question of meaning in your life story, you'll see how you make sense of the life you've been given. If logic is your primary method, you will tend toward a rational approach. If you're guided by intuition and focus on signals from within, you're more likely to be drawn to mythic and archetypal approaches.

Central to our sense of meaning is the theme of having a home. More than a mere structure, this is where we find our place in the world. In this chapter, we'll look at why home is a state of mind that brings feelings of belonging and worthiness. We'll also examine the importance of choice in building meaning because what you choose determines how you shape your purpose. With a purpose, you can decide what really matters and what does not. You can see that certain choices lead toward the truth while others lead toward impostorhood. Although meaning is itself a story, you have the power to use this narrative to elevate the quality of your life.

MAKING SENSE

Humans are a sense-making species. As we move through the world, our brains paint pictures of what we see. From the raw materials of our lives, we connect dots, construct frames, and create perspectives. At every moment, awake and asleep, our psyches are engaged in this sense-making process, telling stories about events and feelings and placing ourselves in these narratives. We use criteria like mental molds, prejudices, expectations, and logic to create sense in our lives.

The ancient Greeks said that Zeus endowed humans with two primary faculties: the longing for fairness and justice, and the capacity for reverence and awe. These faculties correspond to two different ways of viewing ourselves and the world, which are called "logos" and "mythos." Logos refers to our ordinary way of seeing the world with deductive, logical thinking that helps us balance our checkbook, make decisions, and plan for the future. But as scholar Karen Armstrong describes, the ancients saw that logos cannot "assuage human grief or find ultimate meaning in life's struggle. For that people turned to mythos, stories that made no pretensions to historical accuracy but should rather be seen as an early form of psychology."

Mythos can move the heart to love, inspire faith, and find magic in the metaphorical mystery of life. Mythic thinking allows us to ponder life's deepest questions through a larger aperture, to reinterpret our struggles against an eternal backdrop. Mythos is concerned more with feeling than thought, motivated more by faith than reason. The mythic mind ponders metaphysical questions while the logical mind counts the beans and weighs the odds. While most of us tend toward one approach or the other, both mythos and logos are necessary for a balanced life. Unfortunately, in our reason-obsessed, left-brained culture, we favor logic over myth, facts over fables, and black-and-white explanations over the rainbow spectrum of awe. This leads to an impoverished view of existence: sensible without being wise, logical without being enriching.

Logos without mythos can lead to confusion. If you tend toward rationality, and find your deepest comfort in hard facts and precise thinking, you may be someone who looks to security as the hallmark of a meaningful life. If you tend toward mythic thinking, you may find logic too dry and tidy, and prefer symbolism, archetypes, and intuition. You may depend on spiritual resonance as a source of meaning. Knowing whether you are pulled toward either mythos or logos can help you understand how you make sense of your life, and how you can balance your perspective. For example, Seth sat down to write about a crossroads in his life. He was burned out on a job that paid well but felt meaningless. So he gave his logos mind the first shot and wrote to explore those values.

> *The odds of finding a different job that pays this much are extremely low. There are great benefits, it's close to my home, and since I'm in my mid-thirties and want to have kids, I should be practical. Every job brings its aggravations. Besides, if I stay for another five years there will be profit-sharing. And the organization itself does great work in the world even though my job is dull.*

Logos mind appraises what is known and arrives at reasonable conclusions. Its approach is deductive; from known facts and hypotheses, it draws a logical response, remaining objective and surface-oriented. It makes sense but it doesn't find inspiration. Now look at what Seth's mythos mind made of the same situation.

> *I feel like I've come to a fork in the road, spiritually. It relates with personal power: I've played the apprentice, the mentee, the functionary, but haven't bloomed creatively. My soul feels cramped and I can't move on to my next growth phase without taking a risk. Unless I can trust that I will find my way if I stay true to my inner calling, I can't come into true feelings of abundance.*

Most of us oscillate between these two kinds of storytelling. Both versions may be said to be true yet appeal to separate parts of our psyche. Depending on our temperament, we balance these complementary perspectives in a manner that suits our preferred style. Ideally, when making important choices in life we see through both portals. Including both a rational and metaphorical approach in writing and self-inquiry widens your aperture and maximizes choice. It also creates wisdom; knowing that both ways of seeing are valuable and true gives us a greater view than a singular approach. These prompts will move you toward a more balanced perspective in how you understand your own story.

Core Insights

☐ At every moment, our psyches are engaged in telling stories about events and feelings, and placing ourselves in these narratives.

☐ The ancient Greeks had two ways of viewing ourselves and the world. Logos refers to deductive, logical thinking, and mythos ponders metaphysical questions.

☐ Our left-brained culture favors logic over myth and black-and-white explanations over the rainbow spectrum of awe—which leads to an impoverished view of existence.

☐ Knowing whether we are pulled toward either mythos or logos can help us understand how we make sense of our life and see where we need to balance our perspective.

Dive Deeper

• Do you tend to view your life and purpose through the eyes of logic, or the lens of myth? When did you first become aware of this preference? What are the strengths and limitations of your position? What can you do to bring more balance and wisdom to your perspective?

• Write about a challenge you are facing from each of these perspectives. What does this challenge mean to you when you view it logically? How does its meaning shift when you consider it as a step on your mythic, or spiritual, journey?

- Describe the relationship between control and inspiration in your life. Does rationality interfere with creativity for you? If so, give examples.

- Using the wisdom of seeing with both perspectives, describe a difficult relationship in your life. What have you not acknowledged in this relationship? How can you balance logos and mythos in your story about this contentious bond?

When you write about how you make sense of your life, and discover where you may have an imbalance between right- and left-brained ways of seeing, you develop deeper access to wisdom and meaning. These are important tools for locating yourself in the world, for finding out where you feel at home and are certain you belong.

WHERE IS HOME?

The quest for meaning includes finding your home in the world. This home may not be geographical. A friend of mine devotes her life to Doctors Without Borders. Though she's fond of her suburban house in New Jersey, her deepest sense of home comes from being where the greatest need exists. When treating refugees in foreign countries, my friend feels she belongs. Being a doctor locates her in the world—for this generous, compassionate woman, home is an emotional state more than a swimming pool and circular driveway.

A few years back, I traveled around the United States doing research for an article about the epidemic of homelessness in our country. When I spoke to homeless individuals, I began to grasp the spiritual meaning of home and its impact on everyday human life, regardless of whether or not we have a permanent address. Homelessness is a state of mind many of us have experienced in times of transition and struggle, during intervals of heartache, confusion, and disappointment. Though we may have a roof over our head, we nonetheless feel homeless, dislocated, and abandoned. In such times, we discover that home has an existential importance that relates to our deepest insecurities about living on this mysterious planet in the first place. Through this spiritual lens, home is where you find your heart as much as where you hang your hat. It is connected to the idea of sanctuary, as we discussed in the lesson on finding an inner refuge. In Buddhist teachings, spiritual initiation is known as "taking refuge" and is related to this sense of home and sanctuary. As something we create for ourselves, we can feel more at home with a group of like-minded strangers than we do with biological family.

Catherine lived like a cat on a hot tin roof. Wherever she landed, Catherine would leave as fast as she could pack her suitcase. For twenty years, she traveled incessantly, looking for a place where she felt she belonged. But this perfect place eluded her because no matter where she was, Catherine invented a reason why it could never be her home. When she joined my course, she was exhausted and filled with rationales about why no place would satisfy her. I asked Catherine to write about a destination that might give her joy. What sort of home might feel right for reasons she couldn't make logical sense of? Where did she feel her spirit belonged? Which place would be best for developing her gifts? Here is what Catherine wrote.

> *I've always felt called to live on a ranch. That's crazy*
> *since I'm single without a lot of expendable income. But*
> *when I close my eyes and see myself somewhere, it's*
> *always outdoors on a kind of plateau that's surrounded*
> *by mountains and full of animals. Horses, goats, pigs, the*
> *lot. When I think about that, my heart sings. It feels like*

*I could find something there that I've wanted but never
found. A missing piece. But where would that be?*

Catherine had opened a surprising new door. In order to move
through it, she would need to look at home from the inside-out—
rather than binge-shop external locations—and become aware of
yearnings and images she'd long suppressed for the sake of practi-
cality. As the class continued, I encouraged Catherine to flesh out
her vision by exploring the feelings each element of her pastoral
scene brought up: the animals, mountains, solitude, Western
flavor, and outdoorsy lifestyle. What did each of these elements say
about who she was and where she belonged? In the end, her love of
animals let her know it didn't really matter where she was, as long
as she could have assorted pets. Catherine joked, "How can I make
a major life choice based on moving somewhere I can have a goat?"
I responded by asking her, "How could you not?" By the time the
class ended, Catherine had decided to put down stakes in Arizona,
where she became the caretaker of an estate where the owner
allowed her to have as many animals as she wanted.

Where do you feel at home and why? What are the elements of
home that matter to you? And how does home connect to your
sense of purpose? These deepening practices will help you find out.

Core Insights

- ☐ The quest for meaning always includes finding your
  home in the world.

- ☐ Homelessness is a state of mind that many of us have
  experienced in times of transition and struggle.

- ☐ Home is more than architecture. It is our source of
  balance, the central pivot point that connects us to the
  earth as we go about our life.

☐ Home is connected to the idea of sanctuary and is where we find our heart as much as where we hang our hat.

Dive Deeper

By looking at your relationship to home, you touch on issues of safety, belonging, family, isolation, and self-worth. These can be tender feelings, so go slowly through these questions and pay attention to emotional and physical changes along the way.

- Write about a homeless period in your life, a time when you didn't know where you belonged, lacked refuge, and couldn't take root.

- Describe your ideal home and why it would suit you well. What would living there mean to you? What are the elements that would give you joy? In what ways might this ideal home defy logic?

- What did home mean for you while growing up? Was it a comforting location or a danger zone? Did you feel that you belonged with your family of origin? Why and why not?

- What can you do in your present circumstances to deepen feelings of home and belonging, on physical, emotional, and spiritual levels?

Until you understand what home means to you, it's hard to know what to make of your life, or which direction to take. Without such an orientation, choice-making can feel like a game of chance. Having a sense of where you belong helps you decide what matters and what doesn't. By learning to choose mindfully, attending to both mythos and logos, you cultivate a more meaningful life.

THE POWER OF CHOICE

We may or may not be able to choose our home, but we can decide what home means to us. Through choice, we affirm what matters to us and what doesn't. Choice not only determines meaning, it also creates the conditions for change. Whatever our life circumstances, we have the power to affect them through the choices we make. This holds true in both everyday matters and life-and-death situations.

Consider the story of psychologist Viktor Frankl, author of the classic book *Man's Search for Meaning*. Frankl was taken to a concentration camp during World War II, and as he struggled to keep body and soul intact, he made a startling discovery about the power of choice. This is how he described it.

> We who lived in concentration camps can remember the men who walked through the huts comforting others, giving away their last piece of bread. They may have been few in number, but they offer sufficient proof that everything can be taken from a man but one thing: the last of human freedoms—to choose one's attitude in any given set of circumstances, to choose one's own way.

Frankl realized that choice and meaning are integral to self-awareness—regardless of our surroundings. Whether we find we're in difficult straits or in the lap of privilege, this is a universal truth. The ability to imbue our life with beauty and meaning is an inside job. In a universe we cannot control, it is still possible to choose our own attitude and the quality of our inner life. This recognition is transformational. No longer the victim of circumstance, we take back power over how we respond, and learn to make more awakened choices.

To grasp this life-changing truth, we must first acknowledge that choice and control have little to do with each other. Choice centers on how you respond to conditions. Control is focused on changing conditions. While control tends to be outward-directed, choice is always an internal shift. When driving a car across difficult terrain, a control-orientation will be concerned with fixing the road, painting dividing lines, and installing traffic lights. A choice-orientation will focus on improving driving skills, adjusting speed, and being mindful of the right direction. Control is forever limited, and often frustrated, by external factors. Choice is limitless, flexible, and creative, regardless of the road conditions.

Discovering the power of choice through writing can turn adverse situations into opportunities. You recapture energy sacrificed to the victim's story. As long as you choose your own attitude, you cannot be a victim. By taking possession of your own choices, your sense of meaning deepens. This liberating insight can save your life. Use these prompts to look at the power of choice and your skills as choicemaker.

Core Insights

☐ The connection between personal choice and a meaningful life is important to understand. Our choices define what matters to us and create conditions for change.

☐ Choice and meaning are integral to self-awareness. We can imbue our life with meaning by choosing our own attitude and the quality of our inner life.

☐ Choice and control have little to do with each other. Choice centers on how you respond to conditions. Control is focused on changing conditions.

☐ Discovering the power of choice through writing can turn adverse situations into opportunities.

Dive Deeper

This is a transformational process. Your experience is changed by what you choose. These questions will help clarify how you make your life choices.

- Write three examples of choices you made under duress that affected your life in positive or negative ways. Why did you make those choices? How might you choose differently today?

- Do you consider choice to be a burden or an opportunity? In what circumstances do you prefer to have no choice, to give your power away?

- How does your need for control limit your ability to choose mindfully? How does the power of choice affect your need for control?

- Write about a choice that would make your life more meaningful. What stops you from making this choice now?

When you see diverse options, and how free you are to choose differently, it opens your mind and eases your heart. Writing with the intention to make that happen is a liberating process. The story of who you are can change, guiding you toward what really matters.

WHAT REALLY MATTERS?

As we write about experience, we are coloring it with value, honing it with bias, and shaping it to suit our tastes and needs. We are choosing what matters and what doesn't, what counts and what doesn't deserve our attention. That is why meaning itself is a changing story, which does not detract from its value. Story is worth a lot—as long as we know that it's a story. We use our stories to navigate existence as we use our body to maneuver through the world. Like clothing, our shifting narratives help us survive in different environments and conditions.

It's important to realize that meaning is a changing story; what matters is what we *say* matters, which is constantly in flux. What meant a lot to you yesterday may be history today, while formerly meaningless parts of life can suddenly become urgent. This evolution of significance, and what matters, depends on telling the truth. I worked with a student named Flint who was going through a depression. In his first piece of writing, Flint wrote, "I feel like the juice is drained out of me. Nothing feels like it really matters. It's like the pilot light has gone out and there's no heat left. I just don't care about anything. I'm thinking of getting on medication."

Flint had written about his symptoms without touching on the cause behind them. I asked him what was going on his life. Had anything changed that affected his morale? Flint replied:

> *My wife and I stopped having sex because I was so miserable. She blames me for everything. There's no message like, "Honey are you okay?" She's just mad all the time. And the madder she gets, the more I avoid her. It's a vicious circle. When wasn't it?*

When wasn't it? I asked Flint to write about that sentence. That's when the dam broke inside him.

> *I have a hard time saying this, but I hate my wife. I really hate her. She's not a nice person. The thought of living with her for the rest of my life makes me want to kill myself. I've never said that out loud. But I'd rather not be here than be with her for the next twenty years.*

By telling the truth, Flint realized that he was angry, not depressed. As he explored his rage in writing, the blanket of sadness that had covered him in meaninglessness began to burn off. Years of withheld emotions, resentments, and outrage poured out of

Flint, until he saw that he needed to leave the marriage. Foregoing the Prozac, he got a divorce. Because he'd revealed his untold story, Flint's life began to matter again.

Positive psychology tells us that happiness is inseparable from a sense of purpose. To find what really matters to you, look at what makes you truly happy, deeply satisfied, creatively engaged, and useful-feeling in the world. Happiness levels rise higher when we are engaged in activities that connect us to a sense of greater good and causes that are larger than ourselves. The things that matter in our life are energy boosters and provide fuel to carry us through moments of doubt and uncertainty.

After Flint left his wife, he was able to choose—honestly and mindfully—what he wanted to do next. What would give his life meaning? How could he use what he knew as a bridge for connecting to others? In the end, Flint decided to enroll in chef school because he liked to feed people. "That's what gives me joy. Bringing a little comfort to people's lives. I know it's just food, but it's love to me." Flint's customers surely agree.

When you find yourself wondering what really matters, take a look at the world around you. Where can your strengths and gifts contribute to something the world needs? How can who you are, what you know, and the things you care about help to improve the lives of others? Explore these themes as you respond to these prompts.

Core Insights

- ☐ Meaning is a story we use to navigate our existence, which helps us in different environments and conditions. We find out what matters to us by telling the truth.

- ☐ Positive psychology tells us that happiness is inseparable from a sense of purpose.

☐ Happiness levels rise higher when we are engaged in activities that connect us to a sense of greater good.

☐ The things that matter in our lives are energy boosters and provide fuel to carry us through moments of doubt and uncertainty.

Dive Deeper

• How is your meaning story changing? What matters to you today that didn't matter a year ago? What do you no longer care about?

• With these changes in meaning, what new choices do you have to make? What are your obstacles to making these choices?

• Tell an untold story that could affect the meaning of your life if you admitted it. If you can't think of an untold story, write about an unspoken desire that might change what your life means to you.

• What do you have to offer the world? Where does your gift intersect with the greater good? How would engaging this gift add meaning to your life?

Once you know that meaning is a story that is always changing, you can ask fresh questions, tell the truth, and be flexible about what matters and what doesn't. The realization that happiness comes from connecting to something larger than yourself can help guide your choices. To find this meeting point, allow yourself to be directed by intuition. Writing will help you get there, guided by the heart's pull toward wisdom, transformation, and love.

6 Love Invents Us

In its many manifestations, love is the foundation of a meaningful life. The body is the vehicle of human love, and it's helpful to observe the effects of physical touch on emotional life. In this chapter, we'll explore how we reconcile physical needs with the spiritual dimension of love and how in sexual relationships we can cultivate intimacy without a loss of desire or passion. By considering the effects of attachment on human love, and the difference between attachment and commitment, you'll see that they prompt different kinds of passion. We'll look at ways of responding to passion without falling into addiction and how love, in all its forms, requires forgiveness to survive. Without forgiveness, we are stuck in the past. Love is always happening now.

THE BODY IN LOVE

Without the ability to nurture, care, and think of others, life would be drained of significance. Love in the broadest sense of honoring the humanity of others and upholding the sacredness of the world is the foundation of a life that matters. If we can't open our hearts with a measure of unconditional love, then no authentic awakening happens.

As we saw in the lesson on the mothering gaze, love begins in the body. Long before language entered our life, our body began its education in affection, empathy, and compassion. By mirroring our caregiver's love toward us, we learned to exhibit that care toward others. Through the power of touch, our body absorbed the kindness of others and located a stable psychological base. The way we were physically handled as children determines a lot about how we handle others later in life. As we grow into puberty, this need to be touched reaches a new crescendo. Hormones propel our bodies toward one another as the desires to be touched, held, and known increases our longing for emotional connection.

In relationships that are romantic or erotic, the physical body factors into love in ways that can be confusing. What does it mean to love *with* the body? Can higher emotions be channeled through the flesh? How do we reconcile the paradox of so-called higher and lower urges? Is there a way to combine our creature needs with calls of heart and spirit, making the body an ally of love rather than its saboteur?

These questions have long compelled philosophers and psychologists to study the conundrums of love, desire, and meaning. Esther Perel, a prominent voice in intimacy studies, writes that "the very ingredients that nurture love—mutuality, reciprocity, protection, worry, responsibility for the other—are sometimes the very ingredients that stifle desire." The erotic body speaks its own language and has its own requirements and limitations. By familiarizing yourself with the vernacular of the heart, grammar of the body, and syntax of the spirit, you take an important step toward self-understanding: learning to love as a physical being. Writing can help you articulate the paradoxes that this involves. When I ask my students to write about love as it relates to the physical body, their responses vary tremendously.

> Marlene: *The body gets in the way of love. I've been with my husband for thirty-two years and sex has never been our best part. This sounds strange to say but I never feel more distant from him than after we have sex. I don't feel like I exist for him.*

> Deborah: *I can't connect emotionally to my boyfriend without sex. When we don't make love, I feel insecure. It's*

easy to lie with words but the body always tell the truth.
We all have wandering eyeballs. If he can't bring the
attention back to me, I know there's something wrong.

David: *I'm conflicted when it comes to women. I objectify*
them and love them at the same time. I'm spiritually
drawn to females till the minute we make physical contact;
then it changes to an animal thing. And maybe there's
nothing wrong with that. But maybe there is.

Hector: *I'm at a point in my life when sex without love*
doesn't interest me. Been there, done that. If I don't care
about somebody, why bother? I know a lot of men who
don't agree and think it's worth it just to have sex. I don't
like that feeling anymore.

As you explore your thoughts and feelings about love, it will
become clear that erotic experience—in its myriad forms—has had
a dramatic impact on your sense of self. The body is always part of
love, since without incarnation love can't exist, and this is fascinating territory to mine for your core beliefs and narratives. See what
emerges from the stories you tell about your own body in the act of
loving.

Core Insights

- ☐ Without the ability to open your heart, no awakening
  can happen. This must involve the physical body.

- ☐ Through the power of touch, our body absorbs the
  kindness of others and locates a stable psychological
  base.

- ☐ In erotic relationship, the body speaks its own language and has its own requirements and limitations.

☐   As you explore your thoughts and feelings about love
with writing, it becomes clear that love—in its myriad
forms—has had an impact on your sense of self.

Dive Deeper

These prompts will help you identify how physical touch has
informed your emotional life and the interplay between love and
erotic attraction.

- What did you learn about love from your primary
caregiver? Did your mother's body create a loving
space for you as a child? Did you feel recognized,
accepted, and loved? Or discounted, rejected, and
invisible?

- How comfortable are you with physical touch? Do you
distance yourself physically in relationships? How do
you feel when a friend wants to hug you? In what ways
do you withhold physically?

- How does physical desire affect your ability to feel love
in romantic relationships? Describe the connection, or
lack of connection, between intimacy and passion in
your life.

As you recognize that love begins in the body—as physical
experience, not a concept—you can begin to see how emotion and
story are different as well. How you tell the story of love determines
how you live it in the body. You can choose to open in love's direction, giving freedom and space to your beloved or you can close
down, cling, and suffocate a partner. When the body clings in this
way, it strangles love, causing pain to yourself and others. In the
next section, we'll examine the difference between love and attachment in emotional life.

ATTACHMENT VERSUS COMMITMENT

The ability to allow separation from those we love is critical to a relationship's health. Without space, love becomes codependency and entrapment replaces a sense of freedom. And yet, love without attachment can seem impossibile. As fragile, imperfect, inconstant beings full of fears and insecurities, we habitually cling to the people we love. We hold them as close to us as possible and suffer when we're apart. When I spent time with the Buddhist teacher Joseph Goldstein, he offered some perspective on this.

> *We assume that clutching and caring go hand in hand. We assume that attachment equates with love. But when we look at these two forces closely, we realize how different they actually are. When we feel most loving, we feel most openhearted. Attachment isn't a giving energy. When we're attached, it's a subtle contraction, the heart holding on and saying, "Please don't leave me." Attachment wants things to stay the same, especially in relation to us. Since everyone and everything is always changing, this is obviously doomed. Commitment, on the other hand, does not say that things must stay the same for us to be happy, rather that we will abide with ourselves affectionately throughout these changes. Otherwise, we only create more suffering.*

Tina was addicted to suffering from longing in love relationships. This included the people she slept with, and extended to friends and family as well. Her longing story went something like this: "Everybody is going to leave me. If I don't lock the door, they'll disappear. If I look away, they'll be gone. So I'll squeeze them tight and not let them go. That's how they'll know how much I love them." But her clinginess was precisely what drove people away. Tina knew this in her heart but couldn't help herself. When she came to my class, heartbroken over her latest friendship break, she wrote this in response to a question about her greatest fear in love relationships.

> *It's like being in a flood and the river's got you and you're trying to hold on but you can't. And you see them going off in the distance, downriver, and you're broken up inside but the river keeps pushing you farther apart. You can't stop them from disappearing and then you never see them again. This is a nightmare that plays over and over in my mind.*

I encouraged Tina to write about how this nightmare image connected to actual experience. When I asked Tina if she had lost anyone in her life, she wrote about a scapegoating experience when she was rejected by a group of friends after being blamed for something she didn't do. "Overnight, they all stopped speaking to me. Bam. Nothing I said made any difference. The more I protested, the guiltier I seemed. They dropped me like a hot potato. My worst nightmare come true. I felt like I'd lost my whole world and don't think I can open my heart again."

This was Tina's immediate trauma that confirmed the fear story. For the next few months, she explored this story in depth: how she clung to people for dear life, how her heart was obstructed by fear, how she pressured people not to change by focusing on her needs over theirs. She realized that although her feelings were real, the story behind them was fiction—a self-fulfilling prophecy. Until she learned to stand alone in her fear, without looking to another to take it away, she'd be caught in a never-ending loop of dread and disappointment. Eventually I asked her to rewrite her nightmare to see if it looked any different.

> *I'm in a river, but the water is clear and it's now moving slowly. There are people around me and our bodies touch and we help each other float. It's a beautiful feeling of being together in the same element, even when we aren't touching. I don't need to hold them back. I can't control the river and*

I don't want to. I breathe deeply and easily and look at the
sky as we all meander downstream together.

By reimaging her story, Tina stepped from the river of obsession into the Witness seat. She touched on the essence of love, which is the willingness to release a beloved, and in so doing began to release the demon of clinging. We can all do this by acknowledging our fears of abandonment and the disappearance of love. These deepening practices propel movement from bondage to freedom.

Core Insights

- ☐ The ability to separate from a partner is critical to a healthy relationship. Without space, love becomes codependency and entrapment replaces a sense of freedom.

- ☐ As fragile, imperfect, inconstant beings full of fears and insecurities, we habitually cling to the people we love.

- ☐ Attachment wants things to stay the same. Commitment, on the other hand, does not say that things must stay the same for us to be happy.

- ☐ When we release the demon of clinging, we acknowledge our fears of abandonment and the disappearance of love.

Dive Deeper

Are you aware of unhealthy emotional attachment in your own relationships? Do you see how commitment is different from attachment? These questions will help you find out.

- Describe an experience in which you held on too tightly to someone you love. What were you most afraid of losing? What were the parallels between that dynamic and your early experiences of caring and love?

- What story do you tell yourself about allowing your loved ones too much space? What bad things could happen?

- Have you ever suffered serious abandonment? Or an emotional betrayal that threatened love? How did it affect your ability to trust?

- Reframe that story of abandonment or emotional betrayal from the perspective of commitment instead of attachment. How does doing this affect your story?

No one is completely fearless when it comes to love. Acknowledging how, when, and why you tend to cling—bringing about pain in love relationships—is a boon to emotional self-awareness. It will also help you appreciate passion, whether it's erotic or not, while maintaining the Witness perspective.

THE PASSIONS

Attachment and commitment represent different approaches to passion. Attachment-based love stems from the passion to possess, control, and consume. Commitment-based love arises from the passion to bring freedom, faith, and autonomy to oneself and others. One passion is destructive, the other constructive. One leads to fear, the other to joy.

Passion gives meaning to our life, as we "cannot live on bread alone." The drive toward physical survival runs alongside cravings for quality of life, ego fulfillment, peak experience, as well as emotional and spiritual transcendence. Passion helps us attain these heights, but when constructive passions are beyond our reach, we'll settle for destructive ones. As psychologist Erich Fromm says, "The truth is that all human passions, both the 'good' and the 'evil,' can be understood only as a person's attempt to make sense of his life and transcend banal, merely life-sustaining existence."

Passion is a double-edged sword. Anyone who's pursued an unrequited love or fallen prey to the dark sides of love, including possessiveness, jealousy, aggression, or competition, knows this to be true. If you're like Tina and believe that love is made up of suffering, intensity, conflict, and addiction, your relationships are likely to be fueled by destructive passion. While it can feel irresistible, it does not lead to sustainable satisfaction. If you believe that love breeds contentment, harmony, and trust, you're more likely to be animated by constructive passion, which strengthens your ability to care for others and be cared for by them. Consider these two descriptions of passion from students enrolled in a course about the mystery of love. They each shared a love story that was also a peak experience.

Michelle: *I knew there was something off about him the first time I saw him. But I found him incredibly attractive, too. He was selfish, unavailable, and much too young. Also, he seemed to mostly want sex, which was fine with me. I needed some danger and risk in my life. I thought: What's the worst that could happen? A one-night stand? A short, disastrous romance? What the hell, life is short and I'm not getting any younger. The sex was probably the best of my life. I got addicted to the feel of him and, after a while, I'd meet him anywhere and anytime. I knew I was demeaning myself but it felt delicious at the time.*

Robert: *She came into my life like a breath of fresh air. Completely unlike most of the women I dated, who were so screwed up I ended up being their therapist. She was successful and independent, and this turned me on like crazy. We were equals and she really got me. I felt stronger and smarter when we were together. I could see a future before us and making that happen became my mission. How could I get her to marry me? She'd already been divorced and didn't seem eager to go around that rodeo again. That was three years ago and I'm still waiting. She still excites the hell out of me and I'd rather not be married to her than be settled down with somebody else.*

The difference between these two passions is clear. The woman in the first story was drawn to the object of desire for superficial, dead-end reasons. She was looking for kicks and novelty to escape from a predictable life. The man in the second story was passionately drawn to his girlfriend by a sense of possibility and being with a peer. He was strengthened by his passion instead of depleted; it gave him courage and staying power.

If you're like most of us, you've been driven by both kinds of passion in varying situations and are aware of how different they feel. Look carefully at what type of passion you're drawn to and the stories that grow out of it. These narratives will give you insight into the way passion works in your life, how it helps and how it harms.

Core Insights

- ☐ Attachment-based love stems from the passion to possess, control, and consume. Commitment-based love arises from the passion to bring freedom, faith, and autonomy to oneself and others. One leads to fear, the other to joy.

- ☐ Passion gives meaning to our lives.

- ☐ We settle for destructive passions when constructive ones are beyond our reach.

☐ Believing that love is proven by conflict and addiction to the other person, your relationship is likely to be fueled by destructive passion, while the belief that love breeds harmony and trust is more likely to be animated by constructive passion.

Dive Deeper

These prompts will lead you toward insights about constructive and destructive passions, and how both contribute to the story of meaning in your life.

- Describe a love relationship in your life that was dominated by destructive passion. Why were you drawn to this person? How did your story about this romance diverge from the facts?

- How do jealousy, possessiveness, and competitiveness affect your love relationships? When and why do these feelings come up? Describe how you may mistake pain for passion.

- Describe a love relationship in your life that was dominated by constructive passion. Why were you drawn to this person? How did this passion affect your self-image?

- Write about an addiction in your life. How is this addiction connected to love? If this destructive passion had a voice, what would it be saying to you?

Having familiarized yourself with the dual nature of passion, and identified certain key patterns in your emotional history, you can now consider love and forgiveness, and how you can't have one without the other if you're telling the truth.

LOVE AND FORGIVENESS

Love requires trust and space to grow, which is why if relationships are to survive, we need to be able to forgive. What do I mean by forgiveness, exactly? This is a tricky question best answered by looking first at what forgiveness is not. Forgiveness has nothing to do with condoning misdeeds, whitewashing feelings, or resigning yourself to mistreatment. Forgiveness does not depend on forgetting, making things right, or carrying on with relationships that have passed their expiration date. Forgiveness doesn't call for communication with the injuring party, or depend on getting an apology.

Instead, forgiveness is an inside job, first and foremost. Psychologist Al Siebert reports that one survivor of severe abuse best put it this way: "Forgiving is a selfish act to free yourself from being controlled by your past." Your intention is not to let the other person off the hook; instead you let *yourself* off the hook with forgiveness, in order to move forward in life. This is an important point that feels counterintuitive. It calls on us to practice against the grain, as Buddhism teaches, to reverse our normal tendency to blame the other, demand atonement, seek revenge, and hold a grudge. Each step we take toward forgiveness in love builds our self-respect, helping us realize how big our heart is and how flexible it can be. Forgiveness requires courage, a word that comes from French and means "big heart."

Taking the high road in love is rarely easy. But when we come to understand forgiveness as a form of self-care, this awareness softens our resistance to letting go and reduces the desire for payback. We come to see clearly that, as the saying goes, resentment is like swallowing poison and waiting for the other person to die. A lot of people die waiting for forgiveness to happen, not knowing it was in their power all along.

Why is forgiveness a part of love? Because every one of us is imperfect and bound to make mistakes sooner or later. And when that happens, it's up to us to prevent our heart from shutting down. I learned this when a love affair of mine went belly up in a hurtful way. This passion had been destructive from the start, marked by frequent upheaval and conflict, and had I been less controlling and stubborn, I would have walked away after a few weeks. But it went on for more than a year before a disaster happened, which left me reeling and determined not to fall for passion again. I was bitter, angry, and wanted revenge. For a couple of weeks, I stewed and fumed.

I was furiously scribbling in my journal, asking myself what had gone wrong and what I could do about it. I wrote about where the pain was coming from. I felt that I'd lost a piece of myself. I believed this pain had turned me into damaged goods by permanently scarring me, and compromised my ability to love again. This was my story about the pain. Then I had a revelation: I recognized that it was a story—not a fact—and this recognition made way for truth. I wasn't diminished in the least. My heart could remain as open as ever. In response to this painful betrayal, I chose to continue to love my ex. No offense in the world could stop me from loving. I closed my journal and realized I needed nothing from this other person, who I hoped to never see again. This freedom to forgive was a rite of passage, as I released the ancient, hackneyed story about how a spurned lover is supposed to behave.

What stories do you hold about love and forgiveness? What stops you from letting yourself off the hook, no longer controlled by your past? These prompts will help you answer these potentially life-changing questions for yourself.

Core Insights

☐ Love requires trust and space to grow, which is why if relationships are to survive, we need to be able to forgive.

☐ Forgiveness lets us off the hook to move forward in life. Each step we take toward forgiveness builds our self-respect and helps us realize how big our heart is and how flexible it can be.

☐ When we come to understand forgiveness as a form of self-care, this awareness softens our resistance to letting go and reduces the desire for payback.

☐ Every one of us is imperfect and bound to mess up sooner or later. When that happens, it's up to us to prevent our hearts from shutting down.

Dive Deeper

It can be easier to write about forgiveness than to practice it. Writing is a dress rehearsal for forgiveness, an agreement you make with yourself not to be controlled by your past. This is an important step on your journey that's often not easy. Take your time as you move through these questions. They can bear significant fruit.

- Who or what do you need to forgive today in order to move forward in your life? What is stopping you from forgiving? What are you waiting for?

- Are you someone who'd rather be happy or right? Does self-righteousness block you from forgiving? Do you enjoy holding grudges? If so, why? If not, why not?

- How do you respond to conflict in love relationships? What types of human imperfection make you most uncomfortable? When did this aversion begin? How can you resolve this discomfort?

- What stories concerning love—like what you expect, what you feel is fair, what you feel is unforgivable—stand in the way of your freedom and happiness?

When you discover that forgiveness is a choice you can make at any moment and that it requires only a willingness to change your story, you (re)claim the power of your heart. This opens the door to possibilities for intimacy and personal growth you may not have known were there. Equipped with this knowledge, you can see through your myths and take this wisdom into the world as you consider your public persona.

Part Three

DROPPING THE MASK

7 Social Persona

The strength of growing insight will help you look truthfully at your chosen personas and the roles you play in social life. These include character masks, strategies for public self-presentation, and the stories you use to save face and earn acceptance. Like everyone, you are hardwired to avoid being rejected by peers or expelled from the inner circle of praise and social acceptance. In this chapter, you will come to understand how performance and idealization help to protect your reputation and ensure your place as a member in good standing of your chosen group. By investigating what it means to have enough, you can see the ways competition and comparison have helped to shape—and distort—your sense of status and self-worth.

DROPPING THE MASK

We began our journey together with the story of a tiger cub raised by sheep. You learned that until you tell the truth about who you are, you're condemned to living as an impostor behind a mask of fiction. You've learned that the question "Who am I?" is a powerful antidote to self-delusion. It helps you explore the stories you've used to survive, but that block you from revealing your true face. Now it's time to look more closely at this social mask and explore how you can drop it by telling the truth.

It can be hard to admit we wear a mask at all. The most common questions students ask me are "Why do I feel like I'm an impostor?" and "What can I do to become more authentic?" Students complain that they don't know who they really are, what they truly desire, and what their lives mean. They want to awaken from this trance of fraudulence and unworthiness. This is a universal condition that appears to have troubled our species from the start. How can we live as storytelling creatures without being trapped by our own stories? How can we use our brilliant conceptual minds and harness the genius of imagination—without losing ourselves behind concepts and images? Embedded in the human psyche is a universal desire for freedom. We suffer when we feel trapped by our lies because these untruths block us from expanding to our full potential.

What does it mean to drop our mask? Is it possible to live persona-free? Of course not. As social creatures moving among different groups, operating in various situations, no one should be expected to expose her whole self to the world. No person can be everything to everyone, and we compartmentalize for very good reasons. It's unwise and potentially dangerous to share intimate details with a colleague, for example, or speak to parents, siblings, spouses, or children with the same raw candor we use with a therapist, priest, or confidant. Compartmentalization enables us to be flexible, multi-dimensional, and effective as we operate in various spheres in our life. These different compartments are not problematic—as long as we're mindful of how we use them. It's only when we forget that the mask isn't us, or find that we're unable to remove it, that role-playing becomes a prison.

Writing can help you recognize the value of the mask you're wearing and, at the same time, maintain a half-inch of separation between you and this shifting persona. This allows the Witness to maintain perspective, and reminds you that you are the original face—the storyteller—and not the roles you play in the world. Grounded in this awareness, you're able to simulate when you need to without losing contact with your real self.

Every mask has limitations, even the most attractive ones. Joe was a captain of industry who took great pride in his work to bring earth-friendly products to the marketplace. It was highly lucrative and Joe appeared to be living a classic success story, but he was miserable because he felt trapped behind a mask of professional affluence.

Somewhere along the way, I got lost. I was detoured by my own ambition. I got so used to playing that part— Progressive Entrepreneur Makes Good—that I forgot it wasn't the whole story. In school, I studied philosophy. That was my first love. In the name of building my company, I ditched that whole side of who I am. Then my heart gave out and nothing made sense.

As he recovered from a stress-induced heart attack, Joe decided to jump ship. He sold his company, gave away his belongings, and moved to a Zen Buddhist monastery in upstate New York. Joe threw himself into his spiritual training and eventually his teacher invited Joe to become a lay monk. He shaved his head, gave up sex and alcohol, and turned entirely to dharma practice. For two years, Joe devoted the same level of dedication, focus, and enthusiasm to spiritual life that he had once focused on his business.

Then Joe became painfully aware that something was missing from this role as well. On a daily basis, he found himself wrestling with a growing sense of impostorhood. While he tried to follow his teacher's advice to view this malaise as an ego distraction, Joe was unable to shake the feeling that this new mask wasn't quite himself either. He longed for something more flexible than the role he'd stepped into at the monastery.

It was like wearing a costume that didn't fit. I could get by as long as I didn't try moving too freely. But as soon as I wanted to stretch, the costume stopped me. The role only allowed so much movement. I had exchanged one set of clothes for another. The costume wasn't me. I couldn't grow because the robe was too tight.

Joe finally left the monastery. He decided to try the middle way by seeing if it was possible to take what he loved about Buddhism

—simplicity, meditation, and self-inquiry—and combine it with his business acumen to create positive change in the world. Joe turned his attention to funding a center for social activism and a small, drop-in meditation center for the local community. He described how this middle way changed his approach.

> *I still wear a mask, but it comes off at night. When I leave my office, it stays there. I know it's not who I really am, as much as I love what I'm doing now. One day, I'll probably wake up and need to change this role again to explore other parts of myself. But it won't come as such a shock. I don't need this role to give me value. The Buddha said all things are impermanent. That includes the part I'm playing.*

Joe broke free from the myth that any role would satisfy him forever. He acknowledged that there is no such thing as a permanent persona. When you uncover this truth in your life, and realize you are the unchanging Witness behind shifting personas, you become able to play your parts without thinking that they contain you. These deepening practices will help you make this distinction and reveal the gap between you and the roles you play in your life.

Core Insights

☐ We develop different personas, or masks, in life to interact with various social groups and situations.

☐ Some masks are necessary and useful, and others can conflict with our authentic self. This causes us to feel disconnected from who we are.

☐ Every mask has limitations. While some personas are easier to wear, every role will eventually stifle you.

☐ By cultivating Witness awareness, we realize that we are the original face and not the mask. We are the storyteller and not the stories.

Dive Deeper

These questions will help you peel back the layers to differenti-
ate yourself from the roles you play. Dropping them comes as a
great relief.

- Describe three masks you wear in different compartments of your life. What are the strengths and limitations of each? How do you get stuck in these various
  roles?

- How do your social roles conflict with one another?
  Give an example of confusing one mask for another.
  How did this create conflict for yourself or others?

- Which mask do you wear to hide your shame? What
  do you fear about taking it off? What will others see
  that you can't tolerate?

- Is there a role you would like to play that currently
  seems out of reach? Describe this role in detail, including why it matters to you and why you don't believe
  you deserve it.

Roles enable us to fit into social groups that offer protection
and support. The drive to remain on the inside of a social circle is
among our most primitive motivations as communal creatures
who need one another to survive. It's important to look at what we
do to fit into the circle, and to see the masks in action.

THE CIRCLE OF LIFE

We wear our masks as a condition of social life and acceptance by
our peers. Our greatest fear is to be expelled from the groups we
belong to—whether tribe, profession, country, or clique. This drive
to remain inside the circle is an instinct that was hardwired into our

ancestors' brains when the world was full of saber-toothed tigers and becoming an outcast meant certain death. Though the threats have changed, our Paleolithic fear remains as urgent as ever.

If you look at your life objectively, you will see this dynamic at work. As a child, you were taught to obey and behave in order to belong. As an insecure teenager, you probably directed a good deal of energy into not sticking out, not being an outsider, and meeting the standards of your peers. As a young adult, your affiliations expanded to include career and romance, with all the conformity those roles demand. In both areas—work and love—you learned that loyalty to the group or to the couple was vital to furthering your prospects and ensuring your happiness. Through the years, your social memberships may have expanded as children came along, you became involved in political or religious institutions, or took on new hobbies. Each circle of involvement brings its own sense of duty and belonging. Together, these affiliations form your social identity.

But here's the problem: in-groups always create out-groups. The shadow side of solidarity is an us-versus-them mentality. This is perhaps our greatest albatross as tribal beings. Our brain is wired to believe that members of other groups are automatically less deserving—for no other reason than that they're not us. This is how war and atrocities happen. It's also how we may compromise ourselves out of loyalty to a particular group with values that conflict with our integrity.

James was a social chameleon. In class, he was mostly silent and when he did speak up it was always to heartily agree with something someone else said. In his writing, however, James revealed that he often disagreed with the others' comments. He admitted that this two-faced approach resulted from a terror of offending people and wrote, "My mother always told me that if you don't have anything good to say about people, don't say anything at all." Consequently, he'd constructed a public persona that said one thing to suit the moment, while hiding the rest of James in a shadow. This shadow spoke out loud and clear when James shared his internal monologue regarding his classmates.

> *I hate all this feel-good crap, with people telling themselves how special they are for some stupid breakthrough. C'mon! The world is going to hell and we're worrying about our inner child? How can we be so self-absorbed? Of course, I get the irony of writing this in a class about self-exploration. That's probably why I hate myself most. I don't walk the talk. I scream in my head and don't change a thing. I'm too afraid to rock the boat. When you rock the boat, you lose everything. I found that out when I was fifteen and I told my mother what I thought about the way my father verbally abused her. I told her he was a drunken liar, that she should lock the door and call the cops. She told me to mind my own business and if I didn't like it I could leave. So, I learned to keep what I thought to myself.*

I invited James to share this story with the others. Reluctantly, he agreed. His classmates were sympathetic and helpful. One woman asked him if there were things he wanted to say in class that he kept to himself. This was his moment of truth. Would he be honest or would he be loyal? James wrote:

> *Yes. I have left many things unsaid. I can't say they are very important—after the fact, they don't seem to matter. Mostly, they are wicked judgments of things you shared that threatened me. All this talk about transformation— I sometimes think it's useless. That's my honest opinion. It's also a giant self-defense. The point is, I don't need to muzzle myself. You're not my family and I don't need you to like me. I hope you do, but that's not my business. My business is to live free from fear.*

James saw through his toxic story that being honest meant being expelled from the group. He learned that when you interrupt your compulsion to be a loyal insider, you see that you can stand on your own. You realize that you can make honest choices based on self-reliance and a healthy level of transparency. These deepening questions will help you reveal your own fears about being an outcast and the lengths you'll go to for acceptance.

Core Insights

☐ We develop our masks as ways to stay on the inside of the groups we belong to.

☐ Each group has a consensus reality, which is the communal story and version of reality that a particular culture or group believes to be real.

☐ Leaving a particular group can bring greater awareness to the story of that group and your relationship to that story.

☐ When you awaken to your own self-reliance, you begin to make honest choices that are uncensored by the fear of disapproval.

Dive Deeper

• What social circles do you belong to? Which one do you identify most closely with and why? What are the requirements to remain a member of this group?

• Describe an experience of sacrificing your integrity in the name of loyalty and belonging.

• Write about how it might feel to be scapegoated. What do you fear about being an outcast? If this has happened to you, describe that experience and what you learned from it.

- Write about a group you belong to that has a shadow you can see or a known enemy that creates an us-versus-them dynamic.

When you recognize how much of your public mask is based on narratives of loyalty and belonging, you also see how much of your life is centered on performance and struggling to meet an ideal. The stress and disenchantment this causes can lead you to adopt an inflated persona that is as unsustainable as it is dishonest. This is why performance and idealization are adaptive forces in social life that need to be looked at.

PERFORMANCE AND IDEALIZATION

It's not news that we live in a meritocratic, achievement-driven culture that is based on getting ahead and staying there. As players in this competitive game, we're brainwashed into believing that we're only as good as who we know, what we do, and where we live, work, shop, worship, and stand in relation to others. By believing our identity rests on how others perceive us, we spend our lives protecting this image, polishing it to get ahead, repairing it when it's damaged, and moving as fast as we can to keep our personas in place.

Obsessed with this created image and what psychologists call "reputation management," you grow accustomed to thinking of life as performance. "How am I doing?" we ask ourselves each day. "Do I seem okay?" "Am I measuring up?" "Am I viewed as a failure or as a success?" "Do others believe my performance?" Driven to appear happy, successful, and strong—to perform at your highest capacity—you may find yourself feeling like a failure without knowing exactly why. Regardless of how much you produce, you still don't feel like you're quite enough.

Caught in this cycle of performance and idealization, you may doubt your own authenticity. But how others see you is not who you are. What you do, make, earn, or produce don't determine your value as a human being. The belief that they do is symptomatic of living in a *doing* versus a *being* culture. In a doing culture, idleness is considered a waste of time and activities that don't produce material results—including introspection, spiritual practice, and writing—are not valued as meaningful efforts. For your life to matter, you must keep performing, proving, and profiting. You struggle to become *somebody* rather than *nobody*—an effort based on competition and self-judgment. You may succeed in pleasing others for a while, but sooner or later the whole effort crumbles.

In being cultures, it's a different story. Societies that promote spiritual values over material ones emphasize happiness as your human birthright. Your life doesn't have to be earned—you were born worthy. It's understood that your true identity has nothing to do with external markers and cannot be taken away. No achievement, approval, or status is required in order to be loved. This isn't to say that effort, productivity, and engagement with the world don't matter. They simply have nothing to do with your intrinsic value. Being cultures remind us that performance isn't the focus of existence. Instead, what matters in life are loving, appreciating, caring for others, creating for the sake of wisdom and beauty, and awakening to the basic gift of life.

At fifty, Gary had not yet absorbed this lesson. He was as driven, insecure, and obsessed with public image as he had been in adolescence. Having grown up poor, he was a self-made man haunted by a fear of losing it all. This fear kept Gary anxious, with both feet glued to his hamster wheel, even though he wasn't enjoying his life. At the beginning of our work together, Gary's self-description rattled off the highlights of his resume and family life, never touching his inner life or who he was. Gary viewed himself as an earner first, a husband second, a father third, and a person last. Defined by these roles, he had never stopped pushing long enough to look at who he actually was. I encouraged Gary to explore his beliefs through writing, and he saw clearly how one-dimensional his ideas about manhood were—how obsessed with performance and idealization. It was all doing with no time for being. He desperately needed to take a break.

For the next six months, writing became Gary's door into his private creative refuge. He wrote about secret desires, unexplored passions, and the need to prove he was somebody. When I asked Gary to write about what his father had taught him about being a man, he finally spilled the beans.

> *The last time I saw my father, he was in a coffin in the*
> *back of a hearse after somebody dumped his body into the*
> *Hudson River. They told us he jumped but I know he was*
> *murdered. My father ran numbers for a mob in Hell's*
> *Kitchen. What did he teach me? Nothing. Except how not*
> *to be when I grew up. I loved my dad, but the only lesson*
> *he taught me was, "You come from the wrong side of the*
> *tracks. Never think you're one of them because it can all*
> *get taken away tomorrow." I always feel like a failure*
> *inside, but cover it up by staying busy. I've been avoiding*
> *myself the best I can.*

After rereading this passage and writing about how it felt to state it, Gary started to see himself differently. He could write more openly, especially about his bottomless love for his wife and children, whose happiness gave him a reason for living. Gary came to realize that, as much as he loved them, his family could no longer be his sole *raison d'être* for living. It was time for Gary to figure out what else might bring him satisfaction. A month after the class ended, Gary wrote to say that he'd just returned from a one-hundred mile solo bike ride in the mountains of Grand Teton National Park.

> *I never thought I could do this! Take time for myself to*
> *just enjoy something. My wife thinks it's great. I'm*

*getting to know the kids better, too. I'm not so angry and
tired all the time. I can honestly say that I've never felt
better. I still write, especially when I get stressed out and
forget that everything's okay, and I'm learning not to
push so hard. I don't need to prove myself anymore.*

Having told the truth about how unhappy he was, Gary saw
through his desperate need to perform. This helped him learn to
relax and drop the mask of the ideal man, the success story, the
pillar of strength.

Core Insights

- ☐ Most people live in a state of "reputation management," maintaining and protecting their self-created
  image.

- ☐ In doing cultures, personal value is based on achievement, whereas in being cultures, one's spiritual life is
  valued over materialism.

- ☐ Performance isn't the focus of existence, being here is.

- ☐ By dropping the myth of performance and achievement, we can begin to see and accept ourselves for who
  we truly are.

Dive Deeper

These deepening practices will help you identify where you
overperform in your life, striving for unsustainable ideals.

- • How do you overperform in your life? What ideals are
  you trying to live up to? What are the consequences of
  not measuring up?

- Do you tend to be more focused on doing or being? Is there harmony between the two or does one control your life more?

- What is your story about what success means in both your personal and professional roles? What are the performance requirements for maintaining that story?

- If you were free of the need to perform and struggle, to prove yourself, how would you like to spend your time? Be as detailed and specific as possible.

Underlying the need to perform are feelings of insufficiency. Some of these are socially created; they are real expectations from those around you. Others are entirely self-generated and stem from an existential source. As we look at what self-sufficiency means, you can begin to explore the reality that you are already more than enough.

WHAT IS ENOUGH?

Living with trust in your own self-worth is a transformative, emotional practice. Admirable as it is to be productive, challenge yourself, and do good in the world, achievement driven by a sense of unworthiness brings diminishing returns. It contributes to feelings of emptiness that no amount of effort can soothe.

In Buddhism, this unfillable void is illustrated with the character of the Hungry Ghost, a symbolic being with a pin-sized mouth and huge belly who is starving because it cannot be fed. The Hungry Ghost represents the ego's ravenous, delusional story that the more you have, the more you need; the more you do, the more seems undone; the harder you work at becoming whole, the more partial and fragmented you feel. You're so busy grabbing for more that you miss what you already have and can never feel satiated.

By learning to be present and pay attention, we can mute the Hungry Ghost monologue and make way for the small, still voice within that whispers, "You are already enough." Instead of feeling desperate, unhappy, and famished, we can listen to the voice of the Witness and stay curious, interested, and enthusiastic. The Greek root of the word "enthusiasm" means "divinely inspired." To be filled with inspiration in life is the antidote to feeling so empty. Enthusiasm is an eager "yes" to life, an open door to experience. Rather than fearing you'll never get there, make it, or live your best life, you're grateful to be where you are. You discover that when you say yes to life on its own terms, existence can remain evergreen and full—even when things don't go your way. Every time you say yes, you begin again.

It is an ongoing spiritual practice to recognize the fullness of being and the voices that block you from feeling content. To identify these voices, investigate their stories in writing. What are they telling you about what's missing in your life? What do you need in order to be happy, worthy, and part of the crowd? You'll be amazed by how deluded they are once you get their voices down on paper.

Core Insights

☐ Achievement driven by a sense of unworthiness can contribute to feelings of emptiness.

☐ By always striving for more, we miss the miracle of what's right in front of us in this already-perfect moment.

☐ The Greek root of the word "enthusiasm" means "divinely inspired." To be filled with inspiration is the antidote to emptiness.

☐ When you say yes to life on its own terms, existence remains evergreen, perpetually fresh and interesting. Every time you say yes, you begin again.

Dive Deeper

These exercises will help you tease out these damaging messages and how they take hold of your psyche.

- Write a monologue in the voice of your Hungry Ghost. What is this demon saying to you? What does it claim to need to feel fulfilled? Explore how true these needs actually are and how you can silence this damaging voice.

- What aspects of your life are already sufficient? In what ways are you able to experience the joy of being enough? When does this awareness fail you?

- What are you enthusiastic about in your life? How might you benefit immediately by saying yes to things you do not accept and embrace? Be specific.

- What is your relationship to greed? In what ways are you driven to want more? How does this hunger contribute to feelings of unworthiness?

Your answers to these questions can liberate you from the myth of insufficiency that keeps you struggling for more. They prepare you to take the next step on this journey of awakening: to embrace the law of impermanence and the sacred power of surrender.

8 Learning from Loss

There's a paradox to insecurity, as strength can be found in impermanence. Recognizing the truth of your human condition, you are
free to release obsolete stories about what constitutes good fortune,
and acknowledge that what we think of as bad luck can lead you to
spiritual strength. There are gifts in our wounds and benefits in
fragility. In the art of losing, writing can help you reframe your
story about the losses you have endured. This is how surrender is
indispensable to awakening on this writing journey.

THE WISDOM OF INSECURITY

Ajahn Chah was a well-loved Buddhist teacher who lived in Thai-
land at a forest refuge. An American student asked him how to
cope with the fact that he could not protect his children from suffering. "How can I live with the knowledge that I can't save them?"
the American asked the old monk. Ajahn Chah smiled and pointed
to a crystal goblet he kept on the table by his seat.

> Do you see this glass? This beautiful glass has special
> meaning to me. It was a gift from a dear friend. Drinking
> from it gives me pleasure. When I tap the glass, it makes a
> lovely sound. The sunlight coming through its facets
> creates rainbows. And yet, I know the glass is already
> broken. When a wind comes along and blows the glass
> over, or I knock it to the ground accidentally and it shatters
> into a thousand pieces, I won't lose faith because I know
> the glass is already broken. When you remember this is

true of everything and everyone you love, you learn to treat them with special care. You're finally able to see them clearly. And your time together becomes even more precious.

The recognition of impermanence neutralizes the fear behind insecurity. When we remember that we are mortal beings in a mysterious world, we strengthen Beginner's Mind and each moment comes alive with feeling. Acknowledging impermanence frees us from the desperation to hold onto what can't be protected.

Loretta learned this the hard way. A die-hard control freak, Loretta came to a writing workshop after experiencing a number of losses in her carefully managed life. Her children had both gone away to college, her husband had finally divorced Loretta after twenty years of her browbeating, and a job she loved because it made her feel powerful had been terminated. All these things had made Loretta feel important and formed the basis of her social identity. Now, she wondered if writing could help her figure out her next career move, but Loretta was about to learn more than she had bargained for. During an exercise, she made a confession: "I've never told this to anybody, but I want a man to *take care of me*, someone who can rescue me. I can't believe I even wrote that. I hate women who want that from men. I guess that means I hate myself."

Loretta described watching her father care for her disabled brother and wishing—almost—that she was sitting in that wheelchair. Ashamed of this secret neediness, Loretta had adopted a mask of dominance and control. For most of her life, this posture had worked: her husband, kids, and staff deferred to Loretta as the one in charge. She'd thrived on this diet of self-aggrandizement. But now they were all gone, and Loretta was suddenly face-to-face with her own insecurity. I asked Loretta to write about why she believed she needed to be rescued. This is part of her response.

I feel like a bag lady sometimes. Like there's no real place for me. Nobody is watching my back. It's like wandering

the world with everything you have in a bag that can be
ripped off at any moment. I think I need to be rescued
because I'm too scared to put the bag down. My back is
breaking but I can't let go. Nobody's there to help me. I help
them but they don't help me. Especially now. I have never
felt so alone.

When Loretta read this passage to the workshop group, we were all surprised. Watching this dismissive, controlling woman drop her mask and reveal her hidden softness was poignant and extremely tender. In the following weeks, Loretta continued to explore her insecurities and tell the truth. As Loretta's defenses came down, classmates became her allies, encouraging her to expose herself in the writing and get past the shame of not being strong enough. Loretta's hardness melted and the mask continued to dissolve. When the class came to an end, her fellow students wanted to stay in touch and encouraged Loretta to write to them. This formerly tough broad was so moved by this kindness that she could hardly take it in. Loretta knew there was no rescue coming; also, that she would never again imagine being completely secure and protected. Instead, Loretta preferred to live with the knowledge that all things end, and this wisdom endowed her with a new kind of strength.

Are you able to live with this knowledge yourself? Or is insecurity a nemesis whose shadow you try to avoid at all costs? Your answers to these questions have everything to do with how confidently you're able to move through life, knowing the glass is already broken.

Core Insights

☐ Life is impermanent. By realizing and accepting this truth, we can make the most of the time we do have with the people and things that matter most to us.

☐ The myth of security causes us to appreciate our gifts *less* because we lose sight of life's precious fragility.

☐ Acknowledging impermanence makes life immeasurably richer and frees us from the desperation to hold on to what can't be protected.

Dive Deeper

Use these questions to gauge your own insecurities and see what they can teach you about your attachments, particularly the need for control.

- What facets of your life seem the least secure to you? How do these insecurities affect your choices, hopes, and fears?

- How does your need to feel in control limit and empower you? *Note: This question also appears in The Power of Choice. Do not reread what you wrote the first time you answered it. Instead, answer again with Beginner's Mind.*

- Have you ever had a rescue fantasy? Who did you hope would come to the rescue? From what or whom did you want to be saved?

- Describe your attitude toward mortality. Do you live in fear of death and dying? What is your story about what happens when you die?

When you recognize insecurity as a path of wisdom and impermanence as the gateway to freedom, you realize that the glass is already broken. Knowing this is a great blessing. It enables you to find the gift in the wound, the insight behind disillusionment.

THE GIFT IN THE WOUND

The root of the Sanskrit word "guru" means "dark to light." In this basic sense, anything that guides us from darkness to light is our teacher. Anything that enlightens us is our guru. Through your writing practice, as you come to find strength in your weak parts and gifts in your losses, you come to realize that your wounds are also your inner guides. They hold secrets to your spiritual unfolding.

How can a wound become a teacher? The answer is obvious but hard to digest: many of our most valuable lessons only come through pain and loss—however much we wish this wasn't so. Crisis prompts watershed moments that force us outside our comfort zone to confront problems we wish we didn't have. By facing them, however, we reveal what we're capable of. These are moments that crack the story and let in the light.

Awakening and loss are intimately connected. In fact, most seekers come to spiritual practice out of sheer necessity. The awakening path is no walk in the park. The majority of us have to be dragged onto it, kicking and screaming, because life has pushed us to the end of our rope and the only place left to jump is into the unknown. We realize the urgency of waking up and discovering a higher, enduring purpose.

There is a gift in every wound. To find it, we must first learn to bless our own pain—however much we wish it was gone—by recognizing that unexpected power, even happiness, can arise from terrible circumstances. This is a paradox of spiritual wisdom: we cannot transform what we have not first blessed. We can't reap the fruits of suffering before acknowledging this paradox, that every experience has more than one face. Within any turn of events there are multiple stories unfolding. As a mother whose baby died of cancer told me, "No matter what has happened to you, something else is also true." When we realize this, we enter a new phase of spiritual awakening.

This doesn't happen immediately. In the thick of crisis, we're unlikely to see the dark cloud's silver lining. But once the worst of it has passed, the opportunity for healing begins to reveal itself. Even if there is no change in your circumstances, a shift occurs in how we view them. This allows the light of insight in, and the more we open our mind and heart, the brighter this light can become—illuminating the gift in the wound. It burns away victimhood, which can mean acknowledging, without self-blame, ways in which we've organized our life myth around our wounds and constructed a victim's persona, and how we hold to behaviors that keep the victim story true, even when they are self-sabotaging and make us unhappy.

This is an important point. For example, people who survived an abusive childhood can bring light to this wound by being willing to drop the victim's mask and the label of "permanently abused person," to make way for a new story. This means they will no longer be able to blame the present on the past, to use the losses of childhood to explain today's neuroses, resistance, and fears. This can be challenging because leaving the victim mask behind presents us with the threat of freedom, which is the most frightening prospect of all. We will do almost anything to avoid actual power and freedom. We'd rather tell ourselves we can't fly and sit in the cage with the door open, preferring the familiar to the unknown—however narrow and dank it might be.

When I was a boy, I spent afternoons at a stable near our house, volunteering to exercise the horses. I'd lead a horse out of its stall, but no sooner had we left the barn than the horse tried to turn around and go back to his stall. The stable hands called this "barn sour," and it's a good metaphor for how we resist our own freedom. When we realize this tendency in ourselves, it liberates us from the habit of stuckness.

Writing helps you explode your self-imposed limits and move toward the unknown equipped with the light of self-knowledge. Gradually, you'll become more comfortable with insecurity and the paradoxical nature of things, and how a wound can contain a gift.

Core Insights

- ☐ Our wounds are also our teachers. They hold secrets to spiritual unfolding.

- ☐ By becoming aware that circumstances have many faces, we recognize that unexpected power, even happiness, can arise from terrible circumstances. We enter a new phase of spiritual maturity.

- ☐ When we bless our wounds, we stop being a victim. We can look at the ways we've organized our life myth around our wounds.

- ☐ We perpetuate our victim myth to avoid true freedom, and therefore cannot access our full potential.

Dive Deeper

Here are some interesting questions to write about as you explore the paradoxical relationship between good and bad luck. They can help you dismantle the victim myth.

- Describe an eye-opening crisis, a painful experience that taught you an important lesson. How did this crisis change your story? What was lost and what was gained?

- What loss do you need to bless in your life so that it can transform into wisdom? What has prevented you from making this connection until now?

- Did blessing that loss reveal to you that something else is also true? In what ways? Be specific.

- Do you ever feel barn sour in your life? When have you passed up the chance to be free and favored your familiar confines?

These challenging questions can help reframe your conventional ideas about adversity to discover the other side of loss and pain. Gains do come with beneficial losses. The next lesson looks more closely at what losing means and how it sparks new understanding.

THE ART OF LOSING

Loss is as natural as breathing. We begin to lose when we're still children. We lose innocence upon realizing the world is a dangerous place we can't be protected from and that, in some unknown future, we will die. In time, we come to lose our youth and naïve ideals on the path to becoming a responsible grown-up. After that, we're likely to lose lovers, jobs, homes, friends, faith, dreams, and opportunities. To live in the physical world means being in a constant state of loss. The art of living is the art of losing.

Life strips you down—it's part of the deal—and being willing to change is how we survive these inevitable diminutions. I've spoken to some the world's greatest survivors—from Elie Wiesel, who was imprisoned at Auschwitz, to the woman whose husband was killed in front of her eyes—and all of them agree on one thing: in order to live as a whole person, we have to be willing to be transformed by loss. If we resist the inevitable, we're torn to bits by life's endings and detours; if we surrender our fear and stubbornness, untold possibilities come into view.

Surrendering to loss is deeply counterintuitive. Reason tells us that whatever adds to the sum total of "me" is good, and whatever subtracts from it is bad. But this is an oversimplistic illusion. Gain and loss are both valuable. Often, what feels like loss to the mind is a boon to spiritual awakening, reminding us of what can't be lost and creating compassion for others who are in pain. Loss is an opportunity to see things as they are, tell the truth, and set ourselves free. This enables us to savor our life without believing we possess it, to love without clinging, and to enjoy awe and wonder without imagining they will last. A friend of mine who survived cancer put it best: "I realized that if life truly is a gift from God, then the appropriate response is *thank you*." When we're humble, the temptation to bemoan "why me?" changes to "why not me?" Accepting that we're not immune to life's losses deepens our humanity.

Writing can help you explore your losses. The Witness helps you see circumstances in the round, with an enlightened, creative perspective. You're called on to cultivate a taste for not knowing and aptitudes for mystery, change, and surprise. Artists know that without a blank canvas, creativity cannot happen. Similarly, as a seeker on a path of awakening, you realize that without disappointment and loss, there can be no transformation. You come to see that loss is spiritual grist for the mill and that opposition can make you stronger.

Core Insights

- ☐ After a great loss, to continue to live as what Elie Wiesel calls "a whole person," we need to be willing to change and be transformed by it.

- ☐ Loss is an opportunity to see things as they are, tell the truth, and set ourselves free. It enables us to savor our life without believing we possess it, to love without clinging, and to enjoy awe and wonder without imagining they will last.

- ☐ Accepting that we are not immune to loss deepens our humanity.

- ☐ Without disappointment and loss, there can be no awakening.

Dive Deeper

When you explore loss in your own life, you acknowledge that there is an art to losing and a way of surviving life's unpredictability with grace, openness, and fortitude. Here are some powerful lines of inquiry that will move you closer to this awareness.

- What, or who, are you afraid of losing? What stories do you tell yourself about the meaning of such losses? How would they change the way you see yourself?

- Do you wonder "why me?" when painful things happen to you? If so, when does this question arise in your mind? And why do you believe that what's happening to you shouldn't be happening? Be specific.

- Describe an experience of loss that offered gains you didn't expect. What did this teach you about fear and clinging?

- What losses would strip you of your identity? Why would each loss affect you so sorely? Can you see any opportunities that this would present that did not exist before?

When you turn around your ideas about loss, and embrace a multidimensional approach to understanding experience—in which loss can become opportunity, and uncertainty a doorway to freedom—you shift your attitude toward surrender. Appreciating the tremendous power of surrender is critical on the path of awakening.

SURRENDER

In the *Yoga Sutras of Patanjali*, compiled around 400 CE, the author offers nearly two hundred aphorisms pertaining to spiritual liberation. In this text, Patanjali sings the praises of surrender as the prerequisite to self-realization, comparing it to a spiritual passport that can take us anywhere we hope to go. When we relax our will and lean into what's happening, we enter the state of balance and oneness that spiritual awakening promises. Rather than cling to our willful thoughts and attempt to control reality, we're encouraged to live in a state of surrender, listening to what life is telling us, moving in the direction where we're being guided—all the while aware of an intelligence superior to the cogitating, ego-driven mind. Writing about surrender accelerates this process by showing you where you're hooked on control and where personal fears of powerlessness come from.

Surrender begins with the acknowledgment that a higher power is running the cosmos and animating our personal life. Call it "God," "Tao," "Buddhanature," "Christ consciousness," or "universal intelligence," the upshot is the same: there is something infinitely more powerful than your stubborn will pulling the strings of this puppet show. When you surrender to this transcendent power and move with the energies at play, self-centeredness relaxes and you learn to harmonize with this mysterious presence.

This isn't how we're taught to view surrender. In our have-it-all culture, surrender is often confused with resignation and defeat. But spiritual surrender is another thing entirely: a deference to reality itself and knowing that it cannot be mastered. To our grandiose ego this may sound passive, but genuine surrender feels like a burden being lifted from our shoulders. We finally admit the obvious: we're a dancer and not the choreographer, an instrument and not the orchestra conductor. Instead of disempowering us, surrender increases our courage, allowing us to take more risks by being less attached to the outcome. Knowing that ultimate results are out of our hands, we learn to lean in and let go simultaneously, to be totally committed yet unattached. Even when we're required to be aggressive, we can do so in a spirit of surrender—as Arjuna does in the Hindu scripture the *Bhagavad Gita*. When Arjuna resists the call to battle, the god Krishna tells him to surrender to his duty as a warrior.

When you form healthy relationships with willpower and surrender in your life, you make way for grace and balance. You end the war between push and pull. This enables you to focus on your deep intention to wake up from the dream of struggle.

Core Insights

- ☐ Surrender has often been described as the single most effective practice for spiritual awakening. It begins with the acknowledgment that a higher power is running the cosmos and animating your personal life.

- ☐ When you surrender to this higher power and move with the energies at play, self-centeredness relaxes and you harmonize with this presence.

- ☐ Surrender is a path of strength that allows us to harness a new kind of power, which aligns us with the greater good and relieves the compulsion to control what is out of our hands.

- ☐ Surrender allows us to live more freely, passionately, and creatively because we are less attached to how things turn out.

Dive Deeper

When you recognize surrender as the passport to transformation, you learn to welcome challenges as opportunities to lean into your resistance. This helps you open to the unknown and surrender to forces greater than you.

- What do you associate with the word "surrender"? What images come into your mind? What fundamental beliefs and stories?

- Do you have faith in, or experience of, a higher power at work in your life? How would you describe that power?

- Is there something you are currently resisting? What would surrendering the outcome look like? What story would you have to change for this to happen?

- Are you open to the unknown or does mystery scare you? How has this fear played out in your life?

When you realize that surrender does not mean defeat, you're able to move with conditions as they are. This reduces internal conflict, strengthens trust, and sensitizes you to forces of life that are beyond your control. This shift from control to surrender accelerates self-empowerment and helps to hone your life intention.

9 The Wisdom of Intention

Intention is critical on the path of awakening since without it we struggle to focus and find our flow. Without intention, it's all too easy to slip into ambivalence and procrastination, which costs us momentum and power. Discipline isn't a dirty word when it's fueled by desire rather than self-punishment. Desire is a source of energy, provided we know how to use it. By looking at the landscape of your desires, you can learn to harness them so they provide strength, passion, and wisdom.

WHY INTENTION MATTERS

Many of life's most valuable pursuits proceed in tiny, invisible steps that bring no accolades. In love, work, self-inquiry, service, and spiritual growth, progress happens quietly, slowly, and in private. What keeps us going is our own desire, which creates intention to move in certain directions because they fulfill true things in you.

Writing practice is a perfect example of something important that compels us toward an uncertain end. To establish a practice, it's necessary to set the intention and to keep showing up. There are some days when we feel uninspired and other days when we're overflowing with ideas—but intention depends on neither condition. How we feel when we sit down to write does not matter. Writing itself is all that counts. What happens after we show up is, in fact, none of our business. We can't predict how the writing will go; we can only intend to do our best. No single session matters much and the most unpleasant sessions can be the most fruitful. I can't begin to tell you how many times I've sat down feeling blank and empty, only to write something valuable. Or, I've felt like a genius and produced only drivel. We cannot trust our moods to determine the quality of our practice. We can only trust our intention.

Intention is different from having a goal. Goals are things that await you in the future. It's important to have goals, but when we're waiting for future satisfaction, the present will appear to be lacking and we remain in a state of anticipation, of not having gotten there yet. Goals never satisfy us for long because we achieve one and another pops up right behind it. Intention exists in the present moment and is based on being, not on planning. It is a connection with our essential purpose and leads to well-being rather than conflict. Intention keeps us aligned with our core values. However things turn out, we know that we're just fine.

Of course we want to achieve our goals and succeed, but our well-being doesn't depend on achievement. Our intention sustains us. This is true in all areas of life. Still, it is easy for intentions and goals to be at cross-purposes. If our intention is to spend our life with a soulmate, for example, but our goal is to get married ASAP, we're likely to feel frustrated and unbalanced. If our intention is to do good in the world, but our goal is to make a truckload of money, we may find ourselves in an ethical pickle. If our intention is to let go of spiritual ego, but our goal is to be the best meditator in the room, we're going to be at cross-purposes.

The great irony is that when we cultivate creative intention, we actually reach goals more easily because we have access to the state of flow. Flow results from being aligned with our own true purpose. When you sit down to write, remember the intention to use this practice as a path toward truth and freedom. Every time you practice, you're affirming the fact that your life matters. This effort will pay you back manyfold, strengthening your intention to continue self-inquiry through writing as it guides you to surprising new insights.

Core Insights

☐ Intention is not the same as having goals. Intention exists in the present moment and is based on being, not on planning.

☐ Intention links us to our essential purpose and brings no conflict into our life.

☐ Being grounded in intention is what provides integrity and unity in life.

☐ When we cultivate creative intention, we reach goals more easily because we have access to the state of flow that results from being aligned with our own true purpose.

Dive Deeper

Here are some questions to help you clarify your relationship with goals and intentions. This clarity will help you address conflicts in your life that come from pursuing future gains at the cost of present-moment intentions.

• Are you someone who enjoys the process of getting something done? Or do you look for external ways to prove achievement? Do you try to control every detail? Can you allow things to happen organically as you absorb the gifts and lessons that unfold in the process?

• Describe your relationship to writing today. What is your intention and what are your goals? Do they support one another?

• Similarly, how do your writing goals line up with your larger intentions in life?

- Write a declaration of your true purpose as if you were communicating it to a dear friend.

Grounded in present-moment awareness, and living from your core intention, you're able to focus on goals more effectively because you know why you're doing what you do. You're not acting just to check another goal off your to-do list; you're living with the satisfaction of self-trust and commitment.

FOCUS AND FLOW

We need focus to support our intentions. Every human being is born with a particular gift, a unique aptitude. But this gift is likely to go unrealized until we learn to focus our desires. There are many highly creative people in the world, filled to the brim with ideas and potential, who fail to bring their genius to fruition because they cannot apply one-pointed attention. Unable to choose where to place their focus, they wander from goal to goal, wondering why their inherent genius never quite manifests.

There's a story about a spiritual seeker who was in despair over his lack of progress on the path of wisdom. "I've tried everything," he told his teacher. "I traveled to distant lands, listened to a half-dozen gurus, explored all kinds of traditions—waiting for a breakthrough. Yet after all these years, I'm as confused as I was before." The teacher listened patiently and then she gazed into his eyes. "Dig in one place," she said.

Nothing can grow until we choose. Just as nothing blossoms in nature till a seed is buried firmly in the ground, we cannot bring forth what's within us until attention is planted in a single place. Having chosen where to focus, we learn to train our intention on that patch of ground, trusting that the seedling will grow if we nourish the spot with one-pointed care. Knowing that time and energy are limited, we come to view creative focus as a pragmatic, spiritual practice. Surrendering to a single choice, we learn to enter states of flow and immersion, and harvest the natural fruits of our labor.

Patrick was a bona fide Renaissance man: a brilliant designer, excellent painter, natural actor, and gifted storyteller. Though he was constantly setting new goals for himself, Patrick failed to make progress toward any of them. He came to a writing course hoping to understanding why, given his prodigious gifts, he was still serving drinks at a local bar and living in the same apartment he'd been renting since college. In a narcissistic style, Patrick blamed his lack of success on others because no one had discovered him. This is a common myth among creatives: they feel as undervalued and misunderstood as diamonds in the rough, waiting to be discovered by wealthy and adoring patrons. When I suggested to Patrick that this rescue fantasy was keeping him in a passive state of expectation, he agreed. I asked him to write about his rationale for staying in creative limbo.

> *Choices are like straitjackets to me. I refuse to limit myself to one dream. If I stop being open, I'll die as an artist. I'm always changing! Even as a kid, I wanted to do everything at the same time. When you limit your choices, you crush your spirit.*

Patrick had a faulty understanding of what artistic freedom means. Being open as a creative person doesn't mean going anywhere the wind blows. It means being motivated by deep intention to bring what's inside you out into the world. Patrick came to understand that his myth of freedom was a mask for avoidance and lack of focus. As long as he didn't give his all to one endeavor, he could avoid rejection and the need to work harder. This myth was far less threatening to Patrick's persona than tending bar and being a malcontent. As we continued to work together, Patrick began to deconstruct this persona and to understand its origins. He described a dramatic moment with his stepfather.

> *Mom was standing at the window while he chewed me out on the porch. He was drunk as usual, saying it was his job now to protect my mother from being embarrassed by such*

*a pansy: why didn't I just go to New York and get AIDS
and die young? I walked away and never went back. Mom
visited me a couple of times in the city but he hassled her so
bad, she stopped coming to see me. It feels like nobody cares
if I live or die, fail or succeed, but I keep trying the best I
can—even though nothing pans out. I've got something to
give the world, but I'm stuck. That's why I want someone to
discover me. Just tap me on the shoulder and say, "You're a
star kid. I want to help you."*

Patrick's mask of entitlement had helped keep his creative
dreams alive. As Patrick dropped the persona and explored his
wounds, he came to have more compassion for himself, which soft-
ened his self-loathing. He came to see the connection between his
lack of focus and his lifelong lack of self-esteem. Eventually, Patrick
decided to focus on writing, pouring all his fierce creativity into a
novel loosely based on his own life. Patrick wrote to let me know
he'd finished the book and was looking for an agent. He had finally
found his flow.

Core Insights

- ☐ Dig in one place. By choosing where to place our focus,
  we can manifest our inherent genius.

- ☐ By surrendering to a single choice, we can enter states of
  flow and immersion, and harvest the fruits of our labor.

- ☐ Freedom depends on being motivated by deep intention to bring what is inside us out into the world.

Dive Deeper

You might resist bringing focus to your life and avoid making
choices under the guise of remaining open. Focus can be connected

with failure in ways you may not have acknowledged. To plant something in your life and cultivate it until it flowers, it's first helpful to explore your relationship to focus and flow.

- When is one-pointed attention a challenge for you? Be specific. Do you feel ambivalent about certain tasks? What are they? What is your story about this avoidance?

- Confronted with the need to make a choice, are you able to do it quickly and clearly or do you vacillate? Does the commitment aspect of choice feel freeing or limiting? Give as many examples of choices you have made as possible.

- Describe an experience of flow in your life when you were completely immersed, time seemed to stop, and your mind went quiet. What did it teach you about accessing the flow state?

- Describe three personal habits or distractions that interfere with your ability to focus. What are the payoffs for allowing these interferences? How could you change them?

Focus and flow have their shadows. Ambivalence and procrastination are intention's evil stepchildren, installed by fear to keep us running in place. These common adversaries can be overcome with writing practice.

OVERCOMING AMBIVALENCE

Ever wonder why you sometimes resist the very things you most desire? In the face of our own intentions, we can grow ambivalent and procrastinate. These unwanted responses can sabotage our progress and block the path of creative growth. Ambivalence is marked by uncertainty, which leaves us unable to focus or make clear choices. Without focus, we habitually fluctuate between competing desires for opposing things. This leaves us prey to doubt and missed opportunities. Ambivalence can trip us up in any area of life—including our writing practice. If we are ambivalent about sitting down to write, we justify our waffling with excuses like "it's better to wait for inspiration," "I'm scared of discovering too much, too quickly," or "the writing process makes me feel too isolated." The self-sabotaging stories go on and on. This is how ambivalence leads to procrastination.

The amazing thing is that we actually buy into our own excuses. Rather than focusing on our commitments, we get derailed all too often by short-term mood repair: sure, we'd like to manifest our vision, but since we're feeling a little out of sorts, well, maybe we'll just go out for a drink instead of putting in time at the desk. Hoodwinked by short-term satisfaction, we betray our own best intentions and allow the cycle of procrastination to perpetuate itself. In turn, this pattern undermines confidence, since the more we succumb to ambivalence, the less we trust ourselves.

We convince ourselves that procrastination will make us feel better. Every time we deny this fiction, however, we build critical muscles of empowerment and commitment. That's why being regular in your writing practice is so important, because for every day you avoid the page, it will likely take two days of struggle to get back into the flow. Remember, intention creates its own momentum, and when you surrender to that momentum, you find that writing begins to *move you*. The structure of intention that is formed by focus and persistence carries you past the urge to vacillate and put things off.

In moments when we're tempted to procrastinate, it helps to remind ourselves that boldness carries creative power. As we learn to use time skillfully, we interrupt the cycle of hesitation, knowing that the future is uncertain and that progress requires diligence. In this same spirit of seizing the moment, we also stop avoiding our true desires, however challenging or out of character they might appear. When ambivalence strikes, we learn to identify how and why our conviction slackens. There may be areas where we have stopped caring or where we need to change direction. As you explore your self-sabotaging patterns in writing, see each point of ambivalence as an emotional fault line that separates you from your power. By telling the truth about where your commitment lags, you bust the fiction behind procrastination, recognize the temptation to flip-flop, and see how critical it is to make clear choices—understanding that no choice will yield perfect results. Perfectionism stands in the way of progress and feeds the temptation toward ambivalence.

Core Insights

- ☐ Ambivalence leaves us prey to doubt and we can miss opportunities because we can't focus our direction.

- ☐ Ambivalence leads to procrastination.

- ☐ The more we succumb to ambivalence, the less we trust ourselves.

- ☐ Intention creates its own momentum, its own forward-moving energy. When we surrender to that momentum, we find that our practice begins to *move us*.

Dive Deeper

"He who hesitates is lost." As you learn to focus with clear intent, knowing that the future is uncertain, you stop avoiding your true desires. These questions will help you stop wasting time by identifying your fault lines of ambivalence and becoming aware of your own excuses.

- Where in your life are you most ambivalent? What truths are you unwilling to admit to yourself about your own mixed feelings?

- How would you describe your attitude toward self-discipline? Do you see discipline as a supportive teacher or a tyrant? Give specific examples of how this attitude affects your life.

- In what area of your life are you procrastinating today? What story do you tell yourself about this avoidance? Which elements of this story are true and which are invented?

- Describe an episode of self-sabotage that had serious consequences. Focus more on underlying reasons for why it happened and less on the details of how it happened to uncover deep patterns and beliefs.

When you unmask self-sabotaging patterns, you come to recognize the stories that excuse procrastination and increase ambivalence. Like perfectionism, discipline—when used as self-punishment—can increase these tendencies. However, when discipline is fueled by desire, the nature of your commitment shifts and brings increased freedom and creativity. Surveying the landscape of desire, you come to see how it energizes you and deepens your awakening.

THE LANDSCAPE OF DESIRE

Desire is the lifeblood of creative life. Poet Dylan Thomas described this surging energy as "The force that through the green fuse drives the flower." Desire carries the seeds of invention, nourishes the roots of transformation, and enables us to bring our unique vision into the world. Unfortunately, many of us never acknowledge the full range of our desires. We ignore the life-changing wisdom they reveal about who we are and what our purpose may be. As children, few of us are taught to trust the wisdom of our unique longings and originality. We're taught instead to conform and behave, to repress our desires and resist their pursuit. Like truth, love, and creativity, desire can be fierce—even anarchic—and can threaten our established order. Desire can lay waste to our best-laid plans, revealing incongruous parts of our nature that have quirks and unique contradictions that make no rational sense—but are true to who we are. Human beings are often torn between reason and emotion, logic and instinct, and we are therefore divided against ourselves. We crave freedom, yet remain in suffocating rooms even when the door is open. We long for individuality, yet crave the acceptance of the group. We enjoy discovery and exploration, yet cling to familiar circumstances even when they are unsatisfying.

That's because we are multilayered beings with diverse, sometimes conflicting, desires. Our head wants what our heart rejects. Our heart desires what our loins can't fathom. Our body longs for someone who also harms us. These contradictions are maddening but also inevitable since there is no monolithic, single-voiced "me." By exploring our inner chorus in writing, we learn to accept these divergent desires, including those most at odds with each other.

There's a common misconception among spiritual seekers that desire is antithetical to awakening. Some churches and theologies use desire to scare their members into obedience. Others teachings, including Buddhism, are misinterpreted as being against desire and used to curb their followers' passions. Contrary to popular belief, the Buddha did not suggest that desire is the cause of our suffering. He taught that attachment to desire is the problem, as we become trapped by our own appetites. It's wanting *more* that brings suffering, which brings us back to mindfulness and sufficiency. As long as your desire does not become a tyrannical master, or turn you into a Hungry Ghost, it can be a constructive ally.

Denying desire is dangerous. When we negate or overlook desires that scare us, we shut down the motivating, creative force that moves us toward our fruition. By acknowledging desire and channeling it creatively, it can be transmuted into beauty and power through the imagination. That's why poetry is written and art is made. The medieval abbess Hildegarde of Bingen described this as the greening power of *veriditas,* a term she coined to describe the animating power of the cosmos. This ability to channel energy is fundamental to human genius, which is the innate knack for generating ideas and images and then manifesting them in the outside world. Your ability to do this relies on your relationship with desire, which these prompts will help you explore more deeply.

Core Insights

- ☐ Desire is the lifeblood of creative life and it enables us to bring our unique vision into the world. Acknowledging a desire doesn't mean we need to act on it.

- ☐ Desire is not the cause of suffering. The attachment that comes with craving causes suffering.

- ☐ When we deny desires that scare us, we shut down the greening power of veriditas, the animating force of the cosmos.

- ☐ Channeling the energy of desire is fundamental to our human genius, as we have a knack for generating ideas and images in our mind and body, and then manifesting them in the outside world.

Dive Deeper

As you learn to trust your desire to lead you in the world, you will feel a kind of magic build inside you. Acknowledgment of accumulated desire opens the doorway to transformation. Here are some eye-opening questions that can help to guide you over that threshold.

- As a child, what were you taught about following your desires, quirks, and originality? Was there a time when following, or even stating, a desire had a negative impact? How did this affect you? Be specific.

- Name three authentic desires that scare you and three that excite you. What are your stories about these desires? Why do you find them so frightening or appealing? Do you wish to pursue them or leave them to the imagination?

- Write a detailed sexual fantasy without self-censorship. When you're finished, put what you wrote aside for one day. Then reread it and describe why the fantasy is so exciting and what clues it contains about your life.

- From your internal chorus, pick one character whose voice and desires you like. Then identify one whose presence you could live without. Why do these characters affect you in this way?

- If you are not driven by desire, what drives you? Is it a positive or negative force? How has this force influenced choices you have made in your life?

You've written about your public self and the panorama of shifting desires that motivate your internal cast of characters. This has prepared you to embark on the alchemical work of transformation, taking these various lessons in hand and turning them into the gold of insight.

Part Four

AWAKENING

10 Awakening Genius

This writing practice has taught you many things. You've explored the nature of your authentic self, revealed aspects of your story that aren't true, and questioned your public persona. These steps in the journey have helped you move toward awakening as a creative, happy, free individual. Now it's time to turn your attention to your unique gifts and talents, the particular genius you were born with. In this chapter, you'll come to recognize what it is that makes you a genius—though you may not believe this is true. You'll learn that it's imperative to accept these gifts before they can become reality, how passion and a spirit of play are crucial to embodying your own genius, and why courage is a prerequisite to stepping out of a small version of self into a more expansive life. This is possible for all of us, as long as we keep telling the truth.

ORIGINAL GENIUS

Ancient Romans used the word "genius" to describe the particular spirit, or "tutelary deity," that every human being is born with. The sole purpose of this personal muse was to guide a person to their full potential, enable them to bring forth their unique gifts, and to manifest their destiny. You can be a genius parent, fireman, waitress, stenographer, or phlebotomist. Genius isn't about what you do, but about the spirit you bring to your contribution. The great dancer and choreographer Martha Graham described it this way to Agnes De Mille.

> There is a vitality, a life force, an energy, a quickening that is translated through you into action, and because there is

only one of you in all of time, this expression is unique. And if you block it will never exist in any other medium and it will be lost. The world will not have it. It is not your business to determine how good it is, nor how valuable, nor how it compares with other expressions. It is your business to keep it yours clearly and directly, to keep the channel open. You do not even have to believe in yourself or your work. You have to keep yourself open and aware to the urges that motivate you.

Few of us are raised to trust our originality or genius. We're trained to toe the line and focus on security above all else. We tamp down what's most unique about ourselves in order to fit in. Deafened by the blare of authority and the status quo, we stop hearing the small, still voice within. Fortunately, the more you write, the clearer this voice becomes and the better able you are to follow the directions of your internal guide. Radical truth-telling only helps turn up the volume on your genius.

I see this dynamic at play in people who come to writing practice in search of abandoned parts of themselves. Brenda described herself as a fragmented person. She was an unmarried bureaucrat who claimed to have nothing original about her. Brenda hoped that writing could rouse her spirits and help shift her low-level depression. After the subject of talent came up, Brenda sent a heartrending description of growing up in a love-deprived household where her brother was worshiped and she was ignored. When she displayed a flair for art, her parents could not have cared less. "If it wasn't math or science, it didn't matter," Brenda wrote. "So I stopped showing them my creations and eventually I just lost interest. But I made some cool things. You should have seen my space-suit dress!" There was such a contrast between Brenda's downtrodden tone and her excitement over this spacesuit dress that I asked her, "What did you lose when you gave up your artwork?" Brenda sent me this description of the psychic toll that her loss of creativity had taken:

I hid my magic in a box. I hid what I loved the most, my crazy creations, my girl-self. I felt ashamed but I didn't know why. I was just goofing around. I loved to play with fabrics, colors, different materials, and doing it felt joyous. But I haven't touched them for twenty-five years. Thinking about it makes me sad. I lost something special.

Instead of following her creative flair, Brenda had opted for a business degree and a good job that paid the rent but made her miserable. Although Brenda's parents were long dead, she was continuing to live the life they had wanted for her. "Somebody else's life!" she wrote. "That's what it feels like. It doesn't fit." As Brenda investigated her story, she discovered that her attraction to art had less to do with wanting to excel as an artist, and more to do with wanting to help young girls tap into their creativity, to set their imaginations free. I asked her to respond to the prompt "What would you do if you were independently wealthy?" This set her imagination free.

I'd start a charity for homeless girls—an arts-and-crafts program after school where they do nothing but play, create, and explore their fantasies. A space where girls could have fun, give themselves hope, and feel at home away from their families. If I could do something like that, I'd say my life really matters.

Brenda was amazed by how fully formed this vision was when it popped into her head. That's how the power of genius works. We don't know where it's coming from, we just know that something attracts us with a strange intensity. We find we're good at something we never learned to do. We might care about something that others don't take so seriously. It's a current we touch that's truly our own, and it seems to carry us twice as far with half as much effort as other people.

Whether or not Brenda pulled off this idea matters less than the fact that she claimed her true voice, which gave her vitality. The fog of depression began to lift. Brenda wasn't planning to quit her job even if the charity worked; in meetings she was speaking up and her boss began giving her challenging things to do. After four months, Brenda had been able to write her way back from the edge of despair to the glimmerings of a different life.

Genius isn't about creating something that isn't there; it's about uncovering something amazing that is. To be in touch with our genius is to think like an artist, transforming necessity into joy through creative expression. Here are a few pointers on how artists live that can help you get in touch with your genius.

Be Receptive: Artists are receptive to their inner voices and yearnings. They're able to witness the spirit moving through them.

Begin Again: Artists have a sense of always beginning. No matter how many times they've failed (art requires a lot of failure), they know that they can start again.

Keep Risking: Artists aren't afraid to risk. Risk gives them access to a wider palette and additional dimensions to explore beyond what they have done before.

Choose Meaning Over Money: Artists focus on meaning over money, purpose over paycheck. Genius is the thing they'd do anyway—just because they love it. It makes them feel fully alive.

Befriend Solitude: Artists need to be alone a lot. Genius requires them to follow a unique drummer, especially amid their everyday existence.

These five characteristics of the artist's life can be applied to any pursuit. Apply them to your particular genius and see how much they help.

Core Insights

- ☐ We are born with a particular genius that's unique and helps us manifest our potential.

- ☐ When we hide, or disregard, this potential, it robs our life of vitality and spirit.

- ☐ Manifesting this genius means living like an artist.

- ☐ There are five useful lessons for creative living: receptivity, beginning again, risk-taking, choosing meaning over money, and befriending solitude.

Dive Deeper

These questions will help you locate and cultivate the genius you were born with. Although you may not believe that you have such a genius, these practices will show you otherwise.

- What lessons did you receive as a child about originality and following your individual spirit? How have these lessons affected the relationship with your genius? If you have trouble identifying these lessons, write about your beliefs regarding your own unique gifts and how you've manifested, or avoided, them in your life.

- Describe your particular genius in detail. How did it appear? What sets you apart from other people? How do you feel when you're engaging your genius? If you have trouble naming your gift, then write about what gives you joy and a sense of wholeness. Identify why it affects you in this way.

- Write about a risk you took in your life that opened doors for you in the world or that led to insights and personal growth. If you've never been a risk-taker, describe a time when you wanted to take a risk but stopped yourself. Why did you want to take that risk? What story did you tell yourself that prevented you from doing so?

- How have you handled the balance between money and meaning in major life decisions? Are you driven primarily by financial concerns or do you choose directions that bring deeper meaning? Has this bias helped you live your genius or has it been pushed aside as unimportant? If the money-meaning balance has not impacted your choices, write about how your gift relates to what you do for a living. Are they related? Is there a conflict? Or is there no connection at all and, if that's the case, how does this affect your authenticity?

- Describe an experience of solitude that brought you closer to your personal gift and clarified who you are as a person. How and why did this happen? If you've never had an enlightening experience through solitude, write about your feelings toward being alone. Do you enjoy your own company? Are you afraid of solitude? How has this tendency shaped your attitude toward originality and self-reliance?

Exploring these questions will help you clarify where you're strong and where you're in need of insight. When it comes to your particular capabilities and the transformative power of making them your own, it's necessary to stop holding out for what you don't have. You need to accept the gift that you've been given. This isn't as easy as it sounds.

ACCEPTING THE GIFT

Why would we want to disown our gift? What's the payoff for avoiding our true potential? The answer is simple: the status quo, that warm, fuzzy blanket of numbing sameness that we cling to for safety and comfort. Accepting our gift may mean stepping outside our comfort zone, going against family values, changing professions, changing sexes, climbing K2, or making spacesuit dresses. We say, "That's not the gift I asked for!" We stomp our feet and miss out on what we're given and what that gift is there to teach us.

When we learn to accept the strengths we have, we make way for genius to inform our life. This unique aptitude often appears in childhood and can co-arise with necessity and emotional need. In elementary school, I was aware of having an unusual curiosity not shared by other kids my age—I loved hearing older people's stories. I asked frequent, personal questions about the private lives of the teenagers and grownups around me. Seeing my fascination, they divulged their stories, showing me how much people like opening up when someone expresses genuine interest. Afterward, I'd write down what they shared and my thoughts about what had been said. In the second grade, I started keeping my own journal, recording my own secrets, and felt the same fascination. There was an uncanny shift in how I felt whenever I sensed the presence of uncensored truth. I felt stronger, calmer, clearer, and wiser—connected in a heart-opening way I rarely experienced otherwise.

This sense of being more *us* when doing a particular thing is a sign we've touched on our true vocation. This gift has its own trajectory if we allow it to carry us where it wants. For me, that meant starting a career as a journalist and editor specializing in interviews and profiles, then moving on to memoir and teaching writing as a path of self-realization. I didn't choose this path, it chose me. My gift showed up mysteriously then grew stronger, fueled by emotional needs.

If we hope to flower as creative, spiritual beings, it's necessary to follow where the gift leads. This isn't always easy. The mind wants what it wants and formulates its own stories and fantasies about what the gift should look like. When I graduated from college, I was a starry-eyed writer with dreams of writing complex literary fiction like James Joyce and Samuel Beckett. But I didn't enjoy writing fiction. I labored miserably for several years, angry and frustrated, unable to give up my writing ambitions. I put one half-baked novel after another into a drawer. Finally, I forced down the bitter pill that my fiction would never compete with *Finnegans Wake*. After moping for a bit, I missed writing so much that I decided to go back to doing what I'd loved doing as a child: creating stories from stranger-than-fiction realities. My career picked up steam and the more I was able to step aside, and be carried forward, the more doors opened. I learned to let the gift guide me, which has taken me places I never dreamed of. The dream of writing fiction became history.

As you explore the nature of your own gift, ask yourself what it wants from you now. Where is it leading? What are you denying? What steps can you take to bring it forth? By accepting what you've been given, you make way for miraculous things to happen. You finally step into your authentic life and learn to play with what you have.

Core Insights

☐ Accepting your gift may mean stepping outside your comfort zone. When we learn to accept things as they are, we tap into genius as it is.

☐ Talents, affinities, and unexplainable capabilities seem to arise out of nowhere, with reasons of their own.

☐ A sense of being more *us* when doing a particular thing is a sign that we've touched on our true aptitude.

☐ Our gift has its own trajectory if we allow it to carry us where it wants.

Dive Deeper

When you learn to accept your own gift, you surrender to life on its terms. The tantrum of resistance to what you've been given can end. These questions will move in that direction.

- What's your earliest memory of an activity that made you feel connected and excited? Have you continued to engage in this activity? Why or why not?

- What strengths and gifts do you have that you under-value? How and why?

- What gift do you wish you had that you don't? Why would this gift be such a boon? Describe what you would do with such a gift.

- If you were to surrender to your inherent gift, how would that change your life? Be specific.

Until you begin to practice acceptance, you miss the opportunity to bring your unique gift into the world. Once you make this gift your own—and change the story of what you deserve—you realize how much energy you wasted in trying to be someone else. This enables you to play more freely in your life, bringing levity and enjoyment where there used to be struggle. Play can bring genius to your endeavors and connect you to the life force itself.

THE NATURE OF PLAY

To be serious on the path of awakening requires that we learn how to play. Our predisposition to games and fun, to the sporting dimension of being alive, helps elevate our overly serious selves and infuse existence with levity. Life without play is no life at all. "In a genuine man a child is hidden: it wants to play," the philosopher Friedrich Nietzsche declared. Heeding this pull to passion and play frees our imagination and links us to the child's wisdom. The key ingredient for sustaining genius is the willingness to play.

This is easy to forget in a capitalist culture where workaholism is held as a social ideal. Citizens of a materialistic, *doing* culture tend to measure self-worth based on productivity rather than on quality of life. Your writing practice can remind you how misguided this approach truly is by challenging the myth of productivity. Self-exploration, creative fulfillment, and loving others are surely as important as making money and dealing with practical matters. The philosopher Bertrand Russell pointed to the dangers of putting productivity at the center of life when he said, "there was formerly a capacity for light-heartedness and play which has been to some extent inhibited by the cult of efficiency." For us to remain fully rounded human beings, we need to remember to lighten up. Play liberates our frolicsome nature and, like humor, loosens up the status quo so we can surprise ourselves.

Jonathan showed up in class looking anxious, clutching a long list of books he intended to write. Jonathan could sit at his desk for ten-hour stretches and kept a punishing, nonstop writing schedule. Yet for all his stamina and ambition, he would come to some carefully planned scene and freeze up. This road block forced Jonathan to abandon projects in despair and rush on to the next. He believed that the problems were technical rather than psychological and used a cartoon metaphor to describe it.

> You remember Wile E. Coyote? He'd run off the cliff when chasing the Road Runner and then just hang there a second, shocked at having no ground beneath him. That's how it feels when a project freezes. I'm in midair, my head is spinning, then I crash to the ground. Then I chase a different bird off another cliff and the same thing happens all over again.

I asked Jonathan to respond to this prompt: "While you're chasing the Road Runner, what is chasing you?"

I feel like death is chasing me and that there's no time to waste. I'm determined to finish what I've started, but I just feel anxious all the time, scared that I'll come up with nothing. That fear makes it hard to breathe. I have to stop and catch my breath, but when I do, the momentum is gone. I feel exhausted and realize I'm having zero fun. Why did I ever want to do this? All I know is that time's running out. And that only makes me feel worse.

Jonathan had weighed his gift down with terror and angst, and forgotten to nurture the key ingredient needed to sustain his genius: the spirit of play. Hounded by fears of mortality, he'd confused the true purpose of his work. It was not to prove his worthiness or guarantee his posterity, it was to love his writing for its own sake.

I asked Jonathan to respond to the prompt: "Would you write if no one ever saw your work?" This confused Jonathan, who responded, "That's like asking if I'd have sex if nobody was there to share it with. I want to connect. If people aren't enjoying my work, it's too lonely. I want to put my voice into the world. To tell stories that make people think and feel."

Jonathan had touched the root of his calling: to touch other people with his work. Remembering this shifted his anxiety from outrunning mortality to wanting to tell his stories as well as possible: a shift from destructive to constructive anxiety. Focused on his true intention, he felt energized to go back to his novel. He finished it within a few months. Jonathan was enjoying his work again, as his sense of play returned to buoy his spirits in the arduous-if-gratifying process of sculpting literary fiction. He had rediscovered his passion.

Play and passion are deeply connected in us; it's hard to have one without the other. Passion has liberating, enlivening effects, and play propels the creative gift. We do everything not to end up with rigid lives, and come to recognize the necessity of not always being sensible. As the psychologist D. W. Winnicott said, "we are poor indeed if we are only sane." As passionate beings, we need to be wild as well, break the rules, draw outside the lines, and indulge our wayward, undignified parts—the abandoned, freedom-loving self—to keep our spirit alive.

Passion and play are both necessary to the process of creative and spiritual awakening. You can learn to trust your own impulses and indulge them, which gives your childlike nature a place to express. This relieves the weight of self-seriousness, reminding you to have a sense of humor as you awaken to your true nature.

Core Insights

- ☐ Our predisposition to play helps elevate our overly serious selves and infuse existence with passion and levity. The key ingredient needed to sustain genius is the spirit of play.

- ☐ Meaning and passion are deeply connected in us; it's hard to have one without the other.

- ☐ Sometimes we need to be wild, break the rules, draw outside the lines, and indulge our wayward, undignified parts to keep our spirit alive.

- ☐ Passion and play are both necessary to the process of creative and spiritual awakening. We learn to give our childlike, passionate nature a place to express.

Dive Deeper

Playfulness in life is a godsend: it relaxes the need for control and opens the mind to new possibilities. Wisdom, passion, and creativity are all increased by playfulness. Use these prompts to help you rediscover the secret of play and how it can broaden your point of view.

- Do you value play and fun in your life? What do you do that gives your inner child freedom to express?

- Do you feel guilt or shame when you let loose? Does your inner adult scold your inner child?

- What were you taught as a child about work versus play? What stories did you inherit about leisure and productivity?

- How can you incorporate a sense of play and fun into your daily life and work?

When you challenge the ethos of productivity at all costs and reclaim your right to be playful, you increase the desire for creativity and your chances of flourishing. While it's important to be serious at certain times, it's equally important to be silly at others. This provides buoyancy and lightheartedness when you need it. Doing this does take courage, which is another ingredient of waking up.

COURAGE

It takes courage to surrender to passion and accept the uniqueness of our gift. When awakening our genius, authenticity comes at a cost. Saying yes to our deepest desires requires that we say no to other temptations. Commitment to truth can be demanding. Without the capacity to enlarge our emotional tolerance and reach into untapped depths, we may not be able to persevere when winds of adversity blow our way.

Regular writing practice helps build courage by putting you face-to-face with your resistance. If you don't face your demons, they will continue to run your life. Meredith was not convinced this was true. A timid, diminutive woman, Meredith came to a course with the aspiration of writing a memoir, but was terrified of what doing so would entail. She grew up in a Mafia family, surrounded by crime and violence, loyal to her beloved father who spent most of Meredith's childhood in prison. "He taught us not to snitch!" she wrote. Telling the truth felt like betraying a man she adored and the family she was raised to protect. But the burden of conspiratorial silence was a weight she no longer wanted to carry.

I encouraged Meredith to write her story as if no one was ever going to read it. She was willing and dove into her memoir with gusto. Within a few weeks, she was enjoying her freedom and writing openly about her family, revealing things she'd never shared with a soul. Meredith described surreal, heartbreaking scenes and felt that each piece of writing was like a weight being lifted from her shoulders. Meredith told me privately that she'd never felt this free in her adult life.

Then her writing screeched to a halt. Meredith was overwhelmed with guilt over being a snitch and breaking the honor code of *omertà*. This wasn't a rational response since both her parents were dead and other family members supported her writing. Yet each time Meredith approached her memoir, her dread grew into panic attacks. I recommended she take a month-long break and not look at what she'd written. I gave her a list of books to read about family trauma and memoir writing. I suggested that Meredith keep a journal of her emotional process and new childhood memories if they emerged.

A month went by and Meredith came back, determined to continue her writing. "I'm scared but not defeated," she wrote. "I decided to take my Daddy's advice: don't let the bastards get you down!" Meredith started working again and whenever panic arose to stop her, she responded with epithets I can't use here. I gave her questions to answer when the guilt and shame tried to snuff her out. "Whose voice is telling you to stop?" "What is the worst-case scenario that will happen if you don't stop?" "Who would you be if you weren't afraid? What would you write? What secrets would you tell?"

Answering these questions helped reduce her fear. Meredith kept writing for the next three years and is on the verge of completing her memoir. In that period, I've witnessed profound changes in both her character and her writing. She's far less self-conscious and insecure—she believes that this story is hers to tell and she knows that her family's code of honor was brainwashing. By continuing to write, saying the unsayable things, she shifted her identity as a free woman. This is how Meredith described herself in one of the closing scenes of the book.

> *I was an orphan in my own mind when I started to write this story. A foundling in a cold world. I hated myself. I loved my family. I blamed myself. I believed in them. Everything was turned upside down. Now I know what love really is. It's not about covering up the truth. It's about saying "Enough!" to secrets and lies. I used to think that if I wrote things down, it made them true. And if they were true, I couldn't survive it. But that was a story where I don't deserve to live. I'm writing a different story now.*

Meredith's courage was poignant to see. We all face walls of fear and magical thinking that require bravery to overcome. But courage isn't the same as machismo. Courage has fragility and vulnerability in it, as well as a refusal to be stopped by our demons. There are two ways to look at the meaning of courage. Is it charging to the front lines without stopping because we feel no fear? Or is it making some small contribution in spite of being terrified? The latter is more humble and self-forgiving. We are scared *and* courageous, uncertain *and* plucky, insecure *and* determined to move forward. You've encountered these paradoxes firsthand, as you've practiced writing through your fears, and they have made you braver and wiser. You have been strengthened by internal paradox and encouraged by complexity.

Core Insights

☐ It takes courage to surrender to passion and to accept the uniqueness of our own gifts.

☐ Saying yes to our deepest desires requires that we say no to other things.

☐ By confronting our saboteurs face-to-face, writing practice builds courage and confidence.

☐ Courage includes fragility and vulnerability as well as a refusal to be stopped by our demons.

Dive Deeper

Authentic courage, like genuine strength, doesn't require that you be fearless. Fear is a testing ground for courage. Awareness of fear fosters bravery instead of bravado. These questions will help you clarify this important distinction and develop a healthy approach to courage.

• What is your relationship with fear? Does it debilitate you or energize you? Give examples.

• Have you ever had the courage to go against the grain, to disregard what others want from you in favor of following an inner voice? What was the outcome? Did the choice inspire feelings of power or guilt?

• What do you secretly desire that you have a hard time admitting to yourself and others? If you honored this desire, what might change?

• Describe a situation in which you were courageous, diving in blindly with no knowledge of the outcome. How did it make you feel? Now describe a situation in which you chose to follow the herd, knowing exactly what would happen—and also knowing this outcome was not what you wanted.

By cultivating such unconventional courage—what might be called spiritual courage—you uncover the truth that fear, frailty, and self-doubt can coexist with bravery. You transcend the false polarities—black and white, either-or, this and that—and move toward a third position: the integration of opposites into sacred union. Sacredness has deep significance as you learn to express yourself as a whole human being.

11 Meeting the Sacred

Creative awakening leads to meeting the sacred, however we define that in our life. When you open to this deeper dimension through writing, it reveals the universal aspect of personal experience and the higher tier of human emotions. By looking at what sacredness means, we can see why a sensitivity to the sacred is hardwired in humans as part of our survival toolkit. Time affects this experience, and we need to slow down in order to awaken to our spiritual nature. The hallmarks of sacred experience are wonder and awe, and these emotions change us cognitively as well as spiritually. It's helpful to have faith, and by knowing our faith story, we can articulate the narrative we use to explain who and what we are in relationship to the cosmos.

WHAT IS SACRED?

Until now, your writing practice has focused on psychological shifts. But understanding the mind takes you only so far. As you've learned, by using Witness awareness to unpack mental stories, there is more to who you are than your thoughts and beliefs. Mysteries exist beyond the mind in a spiritual dimension that words can't capture, but can point the way toward exploring. When you use language as a path to spiritual awareness, writing becomes a sacred practice that leads you through doorways to a self-transcendence that you might not have known could exist.

Anthropologists tell us that human beings cannot survive without a sense of the sacred. We have a need for purity and sacredness—a link to the transcendent. This link to what lies beyond the five senses has helped our species overcome an animalistic existence. Without sacredness, we lose connection to a divine source—however we define that. Whether we believe in God, Buddhanature, or the sanctity of family, art, or nature is of little importance. What matters is that we find sacredness somewhere and use it to link to our loving heart.

It's often the simple, everyday things that come to hold sacred value. Years ago, I asked a class to write about what they held sacred in their own lives. One woman wrote about a dusty, old, dried rose she kept in a vase on her window sill. Her family members wanted her to throw away. "I'd never do that," she insisted, "it would break my heart." That rose was the last flower she picked in her father's garden before he died. It had become more precious to her than worldly belongings because it was a link with her beloved parent. The sacred is always connected to love and may not have any worldly value. Even when there's group consensus that something is sacred, it's our individual emotional connection that determines what's truly sacred to us.

The sacred connects us to what is most tender and expansive in ourselves. When you write as a way of strengthening that connection, your practice comes to include the transcendent. The importance of this expansion cannot be overstated. We live much of our lives lost in a trance of attachments to past and future, cut off from spiritual awareness. We are rarely fully present to the miracle unfolding in front of our eyes: this precious, irreplaceable moment. Your writing practice forces you to see what's happening now; it pulls you into the present, reminds you that life is fleeting and sacred, and encourages you not to waste the time that you have. Writing can help you locate the sacred by revealing what fills you with wonder.

Core Insights

☐ Writing is a sacred practice that leads us through doorways to a self-transcendence that we might not have known could exist.

☐ Anthropologists tell us that human beings cannot survive without a sense of the sacred. Without sacredness in one form or other, we lose connection to a divine source—however we define that source.

☐ The sacred is always connected to love and may not have any worldly value. Our emotional connection determines what's sacred to us.

☐ The sacred connects us to what is most tender, expansive, and loving in us. Spiritual awareness is part of an awakened life.

Dive Deeper

Does writing help you feel more connected to what you hold sacred and meaningful? Are you using your practice to connect more deeply to your life? These are critical questions to explore as you enter this new phase of sacred practice and widen your lens to include spiritual experience. These deepening practices will help you move forward.

• Do you currently have a spiritual practice other than writing? Describe your practice and its importance in your life.

• Are there people close to you who do not have a connection to the sacred? How does this manifest in them?

• Do you feel a sacred connection to tangible objects, natural wonders, or physical possessions? What are they? Why are they sacred? What do they represent?

• Has writing become a sacred practice for you? Can you see the power of it and feel a connection to a higher, more awakened self?

When you rekindle sacredness in your life, you learn to pay attention in a new way. With Beginner's Mind and eyes that are open to wonder, experience fills you with awe. Awe and wonder are hardwired in our repertoire of higher emotions, and enrich our life in innumerable ways.

THE PURPOSE OF WONDER

Sacredness inspires awe at the grand mystery of existence. The more you write about what you hold sacred, the more vivid your awareness of awe becomes. This helps open the doors of perception, your portals to higher consciousness and awakens you to wonder. As with sacredness, our species is hardwired for awe and wonder. We need these higher emotions to cope with the mystery of all that exists. The body and mind respond to awe in particular ways. Goosebumps are an example, as they prickle up in the presence of things that overwhelm us.

The emotion of awe occurs when two things happen. First, we perceive something physically vast (like the Milky Way), conceptually vast (like a grand theory), or socially vast (like great fame or power). Second, this vast thing can't be contained by our existing mental structures. Stopping to wonder, our mind is changed cognitively and this creates a sense of space, where new meanings, perceptions, capacities, dreams, possibilities, powers, and insights are born within us. Our most ordinary moments become qualitatively different. In James Joyce's novel *Stephen Hero*, his protagonist describes an experience of epiphany as the moment when "the soul of the commonest object...seems to us radiant." When our perception is changed, so is our world.

Awe is the alarm clock that nature uses to awaken us. We need a slap, climax, or epiphany to stop our ordinary mind in its habitual tracks. Writing helps us set this inner alarm clock by preventing us from sleepwalking through life. Trevor was an engineer who was suddenly laid off when the company he worked for went public.

He had a life-insurance policy that provided for psychological dis-tress, so Trevor was living comfortably with his family in a suburb. His life was good, all things considered: Trevor had his health, a happy marriage and family, and time to figure out what to do next. The trouble was that the wonder had gone from his life. "With every option, I can see the end from the beginning. Like it's already doomed, so why bother? I never thought I'd lose that job and can't get myself to take the next step. I've flatlined, psychologically speaking. The spark is gone and I can't get it back." I asked Trevor to write about an experience of awe or wonder that affected him in a lasting way. The next day, he sent in a vivid description of his daughter's birth.

> *You can't take it in, it's too miraculous. Your brain stops and everything starts going in slow motion. You can see every tiny detail—it's all accentuated somehow. The piercing sound of my wife's screams during labor, her clutching my hand so tight it cut off my circulation. Then the top of Mandy's head and the doctor pulling her out by the shoulders, and then the blood. It was a mess but I was ecstatic and my wife was crying and then it was over. The doc handed the baby to my wife. Then she handed Mandy to me and nothing was ever the same. The world had changed. I was a dad. It was pure magic.*

The difference between this ecstatic mood and Trevor's dull-as-dishwater tone in the first assignment suggested how writing could help him. I asked him to write more about his daughter. In the next six weeks, Trevor wrote one emotionally charged piece after another. Here's how his writing practice affected him.

> *Writing about Mandy is lifting me out of my hole. Misery can crowd out other feelings, but when I write about Mandy the love feels stronger than the fatalism. There's hope in it. I love my daughter's spirit. She lights up the*

room. She's the best of my wife and me combined. When I think of her, I know there's a reason to get through this. Not for her—she's fine on her own—but for me. I'm still in awe that we made this person. Nothing's different—I just went to sleep. And I'm ready to wake up again.

A few months later, Trevor decided to return to premed, which he'd abandoned to become an engineer. He described looking through a microscope in biology class and being awestruck.

When you reconnect to your own amazement, the wonders of the world come alive again. Your vision is intensified and so are your feelings of gratitude for being alive on this glorious planet. Reflect on these realizations as you write about awe and wonder in your life.

Core Insights

- ☐ Sacredness inspires awe and wonder at the miracle of earthly existence.

- ☐ Awe occurs when two things happen: when we perceive something vast and when this vast thing can't be contained by our existing mental structures.

- ☐ Wonder changes our mind cognitively. When our perception is changed, so is our world.

- ☐ When we reconnect to our own amazement through writing, the wonders of the world come alive again.

Dive Deeper

- What experiences or things fill you with awe? What do you wonder about in a way that wakes up your imagination?

- Describe your earliest experience of feeling awe. How did it change you?

- Do you see a connection between awe and sacredness? Describe the connection or explain why there isn't one.

- Do you regularly seek experiences that inspire awe and wonder, or do you shy away from experiences that make you think or feel too much? Are you more comfortable knowing what to expect and what will happen? Why?

Your perception of reality is deepened and broadened by awe. Your self-awareness and writing are illuminated with the presence of wonder. Learn to rest in unknowing, aware of how little you actually know about who you are, why you're here, and what this universe means. Wonder requires that you stop to smell the rhododendrons. Stopping to do so can be a challenge, and a hyperactive life can interfere with your sense of the sacred.

THE SLOWNESS OF BEING

Awe doesn't happen when we're on the run. It doesn't happen while we're multitasking either, just as we can't write while our hands are busy doing other things. If we want to feel wonder and sacredness, first we need to slow down and stop. The body needs to come to a standstill. The hyperactive mind that skitters around like a maniac and robs us of inner peace needs to cease activity.

In *Travels with Epicurus,* Daniel Klein wrote about how powerful slowing down can be. A native New Yorker, Klein went to the Greek island of Hydra to contemplate how to live a meaningful, pleasurable life as he aged. He was fascinated by how the Greeks enjoy their days, especially a group of very old men who met daily in the local taverna to gossip, play cards, and drink retsina for hours on end. They delighted in each other's company and were oblivious to the passage of time. One day, Klein noticed that the oldest of the men was fingering a string of *komboloi*, what are commonly called "worry beads." He asked someone whether this ninety year old was a worrier or a religious guy doing his rosary. Klein's friend explained that on Hydra, komboloi are used as a tool to space out time, make every minute last, and savor the slowness of being.

This is so different from our clock-watching culture, where time is a foe that is always running out. By making time the enemy, we turn existence into a marathon race we're bound to lose. Klein contrasts the Greek approach of savoring time to his aging friends in New York, the "Forever Youngsters," who were beating back time by getting face lifts, hair plugs, and ulcers—fleeing their shadows and living in fear.

Humans have lived in harmony with time for the greater part of our history. Most spiritual traditions acknowledge that time as we understand it is an illusion. In early Christianity, there were two kinds of time: *nunc fluens* (eternal time) and *nunc stans* (clock time). Eternal time never runs out, while clock time is always diminishing. We mostly experience the latter kind, but most of us have had moments when we lose track of time: being in nature, making love, reading a good book, getting lost in the flow of some creative work. We slow down and touch the eternal now, like the old man with his komboloi. Your writing practice can also be used to slow down the passage of time. You savor the words as they slide off your fingers. Slowing down enough to meet yourself on the page, you create the space for insight to open. You access a subtle dimension of being, the same one you meet in meditation. This encounter deepens your ability to do honest self-investigation and then reflect on what you have written.

Of course, we've largely forgotten this in our postindustrial age. That's why Eckhart Tolle's book *The Power of Now* caused such a sensation. It reminded us of the present moment and a sacred attitude toward time. I had a chance to ask Eckhart Tolle about his enlightened approach to time's passage. We were sitting alone on his porch in upstate New York, watching squirrels play on the lawn. Eckhart explained, "When we are caught in the timekeeping mind, we think our lives rather than live them. But when we quiet the mind, we can be present. Right now. In this very moment. When we can yield, accept, and be open to our lives, a new dimension of consciousness opens up."

I asked him how present-moment consciousness changes our behavior. "If action is possible or necessary, our action will be in alignment with the whole and supported by creative intelligence," he told me quietly. "Circumstances and people then become helpful and cooperative. Coincidences happen. If no action is possible," he explained, watching a squirrel climb a tree, "we rest in the peace and inner stillness that come with surrender. We rest in God."

This describes what happens in writing to awaken. You show up for your regular practice, quiet your mind, and become aware of the present moment. This presence helps you open to whatever needs to be written that day. It enables you to accept the writing as it is and get out of the way. When you do this, writing will flow more generously, "supported by creative intelligence," and the truth will reveal itself without being forced. You've aligned yourself with the power of now and time will cease to matter so much. As writers, we long for these blessed interludes—which can only happen when we keep showing up.

The next time you're writing, try removing all timepieces from the room. If you work on a computer, put tape over the clock. Notice the freedom that comes when you do this. Be aware of how your mind and nervous system slow down, and how your writing changes when you drop into your deeper waters. I suggest you do this whenever possible and bring your full attention to the writing at hand. You'll be surprised by how much more you know—and have to say—once you've quieted the thinking mind.

Core Insights

☐ We need to slow down before we can feel wonder and sacredness.

☐ By making time the enemy, we turn existence into a conflict.

☐ Writing can be used to slow down the passage of time. It puts us in touch with the quiet, lesser known regions of our mind where wisdom is waiting to be uncovered.

Dive Deeper

These deepening practices will help you stop watching the clock and become immersed in the process of self-inquiry.

• What is your relationship with time? Are you in harmony with time or does it cause anxiety and stress? How do you cope with these feelings?

• Is it difficult for you to slow down? To make space for your inner life? To devote time to diving deep?

• Describe an experience when time stopped. How did it make you feel? Have you experienced this while writing? Explain.

• Have you settled into a daily writing practice? Have you noticed a change? If your commitment is more sporadic, why? What's preventing you from committing? How can you make time for this?

As you slow down, you begin to notice things you've never seen before: details, peculiarities, moments of beauty. Then you can bring them to the page. You begin to think about topics like faith, what you believe in, and how you imagine you came into being spiritually. Not biologically or psychologically. Existentially. This will deepen your inquiry into faith.

THE QUESTION OF FAITH

By slowing down, we cultivate a sacred awareness of life in the present moment. This leads us to wonder about the nature of existence itself and how the universe was created; in other words, the question of faith. In the same way that each of us has a biological creation myth about the family that brought us into the world, we also carry a spiritual creation myth about the genesis of life itself.

Faith points to our personal story about the metaphysical realm; it is the existential narrative that buoys us up in times of darkness. This story may rely on articles of faith put forth by an organized religion. Or our faith narrative may be more open-ended and secular, free of allegiance to a creator God, yet open to the power of mystery. Faith can have more to do with trust than dogma. The Bengali poet Rabindranath Tagore wrote, "Faith is the bird that feels the light and sings when the dawn is still dark." He was pointing to faith as surrender to what we do not know.

Scott was struggling with a crisis of faith. He was a lapsed Catholic, living in a happy, long-term, gay relationship. While once devoted to the church, he had left it to be a freelance seeker, sampling various spiritual traditions, but was having a hard time finding one that fit. When I asked Scott to describe his own core beliefs, he was at a loss at first.

> I was raised with a rigid ideology and rituals for every
> occasion. I loved them all when I was a kid! The Eucharist,
> the prayers, the incense. I was an altar boy and sang in the
> choir. The church was a magical place to me. My stairway
> to Heaven. But then I realized I was gay—an abomination
> in their eyes—and had to become an apostate. This left a
> gigantic hole in my life that's yet to be filled.

I asked Scott to elaborate on the details of his personal faith—not his relationship to the church. This time, his writing was more penetrating.

> *All of us are children of God. No one and nothing is a mistake. I have faith that we all have a place at the table and that anything that contradicts love cannot come from God. How does life reproduce on planet earth? Through love. How do you help someone heal when they're hurting? Through love. So God and love must be one and the same. When I look at my husband with an open heart, that must be God coming through me. That's the only thing I believe in, but I need a faith community. I want to worship with other people. Jesus said, "Where two or three gather in my name, there am I." That's what I want more than anything.*

I asked Scott to write about what was stopping him from seeking out such a community. That's when the plot thickened: Scott's husband was also a lapsed Catholic, but Ed was bitter toward any institution that rejected his lifestyle. He had vowed never to set foot in a church again, which put Scott in the difficult position of having to choose between loyalty to his husband and his longing for spiritual connection. "I feel guilty because I'm jonesing for Jesus but Ed is so antiestablishment. I can't imagine going back to church without him. Home is what I need right now but how could it feel like home without him?"

To Scott, faith and home represented two different kinds of family. He didn't know how to integrate the two without sacrificing something, or someone, he loved. I suggested he respond to this writing prompt: "Is there a third position that might satisfy both kinds of belonging?" Scott's answer surprised me.

> *Your question filled me with shame and self-judgment. When I asked myself point-blank what's really bothering me, it turned out that it wasn't about Ed at all. It's not that*

I can't feel at home in a church if he's not with me. I can't feel at home in a church that isn't Catholic! That's what I miss most—those rituals, those prayers, that atmosphere. The bottom line is that I have a hunger that my husband can't satisfy and doesn't share. Ed can make his own decisions; I'm going to find a church that will have me. My faith is still there, but it needs a context.

This realization was a godsend for Scott, clarifying his questions about faith and dispelling the myth that Ed's lack of interest was Scott's central problem. The last time I heard from Scott, he was "auditioning" a couple of Catholic churches where his lifestyle wouldn't be an obstacle.

Everyone has faith in something. Some put their faith in science. Others have faith in the power of art, or nature, or what the poet John Keats called "the holiness of the Heart's affections." There's a story about a disciple who went to a spiritual teacher and lamented the absence of faith in his life. He'd been praying for a sign or vision to help him through his spiritual crisis. When he expressed his hopelessness to the teacher, she smiled and asked him, "What do you most love in this world?"

"My granddaughter," the man replied.

The teacher instructed him to use his love for the granddaughter as a channel for faith. "When the heart is open, God can enter. See your granddaughter as a messenger of God and your love for her as the proof of your faith." The disciple followed his teacher's advice and felt the weight of self-doubt fall away.

Whatever you love is a doorway to faith, regardless of your stance on religion. If you step through that door, you'll find what you are looking for: the courage to live with an open heart and to meet each day as a new beginning. These prompts will deepen your understanding of what faith means to you and how it is connected to love.

Core Insights

☐ In the same way that each of us carries a biological creation myth about the family that brought us into the world, we also hold a spiritual creation myth about the genesis of life itself. This has a lot to do with how we relate with faith.

☐ Faith points to our personal story about the metaphysical realm, the existential narrative that buoys us up in times of darkness.

☐ Whether atheist or true believer, traditionalist or freelance seeker, everyone has faith in something.

☐ Whatever we love is a doorway to faith, regardless of our stance on religion.

Dive Deeper

These are profound questions to explore. You are in the presence of mystery when you write about faith, touching on the eternal. Let yourself dive deep in this inquiry and see where the questions lead you.

• What are your stories about faith and creation? Are they the same stories you were taught as a child, or have they changed over time? Why? Do you have faith in your story about creation? Explain.

• Do you use faith as part of your coping toolkit? Why or why not? Do you rely on intellect, judgment, and decision-making skills to get you through life?

• Have you ever questioned your faith? What happened and what was the result?

- Describe a situation in which faith got you through a difficult time. Describe the feelings that this faith gave you.

Faith lights the way in times of confusion. Whether you believe in God, Buddhanature, or a prevailing goodness in human nature, faith is a necessary power that uplifts you in the face of the unknown. Faith gives you the courage to try again after you've been knocked down, and stay curious about what's coming next. It reminds you of life's cyclical nature, with daylight coming after night's darkness, giving you a new day to begin again. This is the faith you can carry with you for the final phase of this journey, as you harness the power of new beginnings.

12 Begin Again

You have explored genius and faith—spiritual powers that move you through your life, which you neither create nor control. With this final lap of a writing adventure that never ends, you will integrate the lessons learned and prepare to continue this practice as you move forward on your life journey.

The art of self-reinvention becomes possible once you know that your stories aren't you. This inspires the challenge of taking a deep look at any resistance to personal freedom that may still be blocking your way. Removing these blocks enables you to reap benefits from the insights you've sown and bring them into day-to-day practice. Awakening is an ongoing process that requires a willingness to continue learning and cultivating Beginner's Mind.

SELF-REINVENTION

It's impossible to live in the world without playing roles and telling stories. But you now know these stories are not who you are. The self-knowledge you've gained enables you to use various roles and narratives in life—to live amongst others and explore your potential—without being bamboozled by them. This half-inch of distance between self and story makes it possible for you to live with greater creative freedom as you expand your inner and outer horizons. This is how to live like an artist.

I tell students who want to write memoir that, until they can see themselves as a character in the narrative, they won't be able to tell the whole story truthfully. They'll be too identified with the narrator to be capable of objectivity, which always produces poor writing. There's nothing more off-putting than a memoirist doing somersaults on the page to preserve his own ego or reputation. The same thing goes for real life. Folks who believe the story are constantly trying to polish their image and manipulate other people's perceptions. They're victims of their own PR. Often they're rigid, self-defensive, and paranoid about the truth getting out. It's no surprise that people like this are often scared off by transformative writing practice. On the other hand, individuals who recognize they're playing a role are more authentic and easygoing. Ironically, they also tend to play their roles better. Knowing the story is self-invented makes them more flexible, objective, open, and able to adapt to the world.

When we drop the masks and set ourselves free, we realize how much choice we have. We increase the power of reinvention as we find more rewarding roles to play in life. Lillibet was a person like that. She came from a good family in the American South and married a powerful member of her community, a man she admired, feared, and lusted after in equal measure. Lillibet struggled to hold his attention but could not prevent his incessant affairs from happening under her nose. Once their two children came along, she turned her focus on them and the sexual issues with her husband intensified. To soothe her loneliness, she found herself overeating, gaining weight, and suffering further scorn from her philandering husband. She blamed herself and decided to take desperate measures. "I did what any respectable housewife in Nashville does when her husband is screwing around. I got a tummy tuck and a boob job. I thought if I changed the outside, then the inside would take care of itself. Wrong!"

The surgery went badly and required a second procedure, both of which Lillibet planned while her husband was away on business. By the time he returned, she was mending nicely, and blamed the bandages on a bike accident. She'd sworn her teenage daughters to secrecy ("It's a present for Daddy"), and when Lillibet was finally well enough to invite him back into bed, her husband complimented her on the weight loss without looking too closely at her scars. Their intimate life improved for a while and he even bragged about his beautiful wife to friends. But instead of being flattered by his attention, Lillibet felt like a fake and began to withdraw her affection from him. By the time she came to class, she was at her wit's end.

> *I created this new me and now she's my nemesis. When he touches me, I can't feel anything because he's not touching me. He's touching this Frankenstein body I bought. I hate her and I hate myself for what I've done. What kind of an example am I setting for my daughters? I always told them to be independent! Now it's like, if a man doesn't want you, go in for lipo? It's everything I don't believe in as a woman. But I was brought up to be a Southern wife and I lost myself in that role. I need to find my way back.*

I asked Lillibet to elaborate on what she meant by "find my way back." Her answer offered a way forward.

> *When I was a little girl, Mama used to tell me: don't let any man make you into something you aren't. She and Papa had a good marriage but only because she kept her mouth shut. She told me it was easier than fighting. Mama wanted me to speak my mind though, and encouraged me to express myself. That's when I started a journal. I did that for many years. When I got to high school and wanted boys to like me, I started to lose myself. I became one of those pretty girls who'd do anything to be popular. That's when I met my husband. If I could find my way back, I would return to the girl I was before. With all that self-belief. Someone who didn't keep her mouth shut. I really miss that spunky girl.*

I suggested that this little girl was still inside her, waiting to be heard. Over the course of the next four months, Lillibet wrote about the fears and beliefs that had led her astray, using the voice of this wise little girl. In time, she told her husband the truth about the surgeries and the desperation to get his attention that had driven her to reshape her body. She expressed how humiliated she was over his sleeping around, his lies, and his rejections. Lillibet also apologized to her daughters for not walking all the talk about being an empowered woman who accepted herself for who she was. In turn, she began to forgive herself for reacting as she had to the pain in her marriage.

Lillibet filed for divorce—to the shock of her husband—and moved across country with the girls. She even had the breast surgery reversed. "I can't blame my husband for my mistakes. I needed to stop the secrets and lies, including my own horrendous self-image, and admit that this was my responsibility. Once I got that, I took my power back. Writing helped to make it real. I'm back to keeping a journal again."

When Lillibet gained objectivity and separated herself from the character she was playing, she could rewrite her narrative and consciously choose who she wanted to be. No longer powerlessness, Lillibet was able to invent a new trajectory for herself. We all have this same capacity, every day of our lives, with a half-inch of objectivity. Use the objectivity of the Witness as you write about self-reinvention in these deepening practices.

Core Insights

- ☐ When we know that our story is self-invented, it makes us more flexible, objective, open, and able to adapt to the world.

- ☐ Distance between self and story makes it possible for us to live with greater creative freedom to expand our inner and outer horizons.

- ☐ Self-reinventions can help us abandon obsolete roles.

☐ By recognizing the characters we play, we are able to improve our lives. By gaining objectivity, we can rewrite our narrative and consciously choose who we want to be.

Dive Deeper

These deepening practices will help you explore the characters and roles you play, and the ways in which they could be updated.

- What have you learned about the roles you play? Which ones suit you, which are passé? Inventory the strengths and weaknesses of these roles.

- Write about a specific situation in which you played a role that caused you unhappiness. How did you adapt the role? If you abandoned the role, how did you do this? If not, why not?

- In what areas of your life would you like to reinvent yourself? Explain why and explore how this could happen. What choices would you need to make?

- Is there a role you would like to play—partner, artist, seeker, writer—that you have trouble stepping into? Where might this aspiration guide you?

The realization that you are not your story enables you to reinvent that story. Using mindfulness, aspiration, passion, and moral compass, you can revise the roles you play with verve and imagination. This provides you with enormous freedom—a great roar of freedom that's more resounding than you believed possible. Much as you may long for this freedom, it can be frightening to the scared self, who'd rather cling to the wreckage than swim in a new direction. This is the challenge you face as you confront the promise of freedom and new beginnings.

THE PROMISE OF FREEDOM

It's not that the truth sets us free, exactly. What sets us free is the willingness to speak the truth, to break the silence, to hold nothing back. Even if we speak it only to ourselves, the moment we tell the untold story, silence loses its power to stop us. We regain the freedom that was ours to begin with. To free ourselves, it's necessary to expose the parts that don't want to be free. You've been doing that with these lessons, examining where you've been less than honest. Sometimes we prefer our familiar enclosures to the risk of open spaces, like the barn-sour horse that turns back to its stall instead of hitting the open trail. When you write, you affirm that freedom is a choice you're called on to make, again and again.

In one workshop, I asked a group to write about their fear of freedom. Here is what a retired medical doctor read to the class.

> *When I'm not writing, fear creeps in. It's not freedom that*
> *scares me. It's forgetting who I am, going on automatic,*
> *getting too comfortable, going to sleep, like I did for most of*
> *my life. This writing keeps me honest. When I miss a day*
> *of writing now, I feel off-kilter and out of sorts. Less free*
> *inside myself, more plugged into the stress around me.*

"Less free inside myself" is a phrase that hits the nail on the head. The focus is not on external change as much as recognizing that you have the power to liberate your mind and heart using the gift of self-inquiry. You can always ask yourself questions. "Who is afraid?" "Who is anxious?" "What is the truth in this present moment?" Questions like these free the mind and stabilize you in the throes of emotion and uncertainty. This retired doctor embraced the freedom and clarity that writing brings. Others run in the opposite direction.

Ben came to class in a bad way. His wife had left him quite suddenly after ten years of marriage. In addition, Ben was suffering from a stress-related skin condition that caused him severe embarrassment. This quiet man sat in the back of the room, wearing a long-sleeved shirt and avoiding eye contact with his classmates. When asked to describe himself in writing, using twenty-five words or less, this is what he wrote: "Namby pamby. Fish nor fowl. Forgettable, cold to the touch, scaly, powerless. Stupid. Loving. Intelligent, not in ways that matter. Toothless. Frightened. Feeling lost. Sad."

I asked Ben to write about his core fear—the thing he dreaded most. I expected he would write about rejection, loneliness, or failure, but I was wrong. "The past is what scares me most," he admitted.

> *Doors that shouldn't be opened, corners that can't be looked at too close. I'm terrified of the things I don't know, and barely remember anything before the age of twelve. Why should I dig up those ghosts at this point? Why can't I just get over it? It used to drive my wife Marcia crazy. She begged me to go see a shrink. But I wouldn't do it. That was what killed the marriage in the end. I refused to budge and Marcia took it personally. She didn't understand that I wanted to protect her from all that garbage because I loved her. I could never protect myself but why make her suffer?*

I asked Ben to elaborate on what he meant by, "I could never protect myself…" It was then that he revealed the true story.

> *I used to get bullied constantly. Once, this kid knocked my front teeth out with his fists. Something about me just screamed "victim." From the time I was in second grade, I got beaten up all the time. My parents did nothing to stop it. Dad told me to man up and told my mother it was her fault I was a mama's boy—I needed to fight my own battles. I knew I was really alone. Later, I started stealing pain meds from my grandmother's purse. By the time I was fifteen, I was an over-the-counter junkie. I didn't care if I*

got beat up, I even used to taunt them sometimes. In
college, I was high almost all the time and basically a
shut-in. I met Marcia in my senior year and it was like a
miracle that we fell for each other. Both of us were
wounded people. She was pretty overweight at the time but
I didn't care. I was crazy about her. She seemed to accept
me too, even though I was damaged goods.

Sad as this confession was, it had a positive effect on Ben's confidence. He grew friendlier to the others in class and even read his work out loud. For the first time, he wore a short-sleeved shirt that revealed the eczema on his arms. He seemed far more at ease in his own skin. Ben wrote about his rage toward his father and his own "cowardly" behavior. He wrote about why he loved narcotics and how he stopped, cold turkey, when supplies ran out and he was too scared to ask a doctor for his own prescription. Ben wrote about falling in love with Marcia, and what it meant to be close to another person for the first time in his life. Near the end of the nine-week course, he'd made enough progress to write, "I'm starting to think I'm okay. I have human problems, not freak problems. Kids get bullied. Teenagers get acne and people get divorced. It's not the end of the world." Ben's revelations were an inspiration to all of us. And then, a week before the class ended, Ben disappeared.

I was concerned and called him. When he finally got back to me, Ben explained why he dropped out. After he'd made so much progress and was feeling better, he couldn't handle the positive feelings. Overcome with anxiety, Ben couldn't resist getting high. He'd managed to score a bottle of painkillers from a dealer in his apartment building and wound up in an emergency room. He'd been forced to ask Marcia to pick him up at the hospital, adding to the humiliation. Ben felt that he was back where he'd started, feeling lousy, living with his parents. He was leaving for rehab that weekend but Marcia didn't want to see him. He believed that he'd finally bottomed out.

Having glimpsed his freedom, Ben had plunged back in darkness. Writing had helped him reach the threshold of well-being, but he wasn't ready to leave his dark room. This can happen in the writing process. Self-inquiry accelerates emotional change and leads you to the next step in healing, but cannot force you to continue. Writing could take Ben just so far, but until he dealt with his addiction, his healing could not progress. Ben needed to do serious recovery work in a setting designed to cure his disease. The last time I heard from him, Ben sounded cautiously optimistic.

They say you're only as sick as your secrets. My whole life was a book I never wanted to open. That started to change when I discovered writing. It was such a relief to finally admit what was going on with me. Like a honeymoon period, that's how it felt, and I got cocky. Even though I was miserable, I was even more scared to be happy. And free. Now, I know it's a day at a time. I hope I can stick to my program. Marcia is being supportive, more than I hoped for. She tells me that I'm a fighter and I can do it. On good days, I believe her.

I do trust that Ben will find his way. He's made a great deal of headway toward the truth and is no longer fooled by his life myth. Setbacks are bound to happen as we approach freedom; the closer we get to awakening, the more our shadow will rise up to stop us. This is proof of progress—not a sign of failure. Freedom isn't served on a silver platter. It needs to be earned. And after we do that, nothing is the same as before.

Core Insights

☐ It's not that the truth sets us free. It's the willingness to speak the truth, to break the silence, hold nothing back. Even if we only tell ourselves.

☐ When we write, we affirm that freedom is a choice we're called on to make, again and again.

☐ In the writing process, self-inquiry accelerates emotional change and leads us to the next step in healing.

☐ Setbacks happen as we move closer toward freedom. The nearer we get to insight, the more our shadow will rise up to stop us. This is proof of progress.

Dive Deeper

It's helpful to be aware of your ambivalence toward freedom. Look at areas of your life where you may prefer entrapment and choicelessness. Honestly explore how you feel about the promise of freedom, both its pros and its cons.

- Describe an experience of increased honesty and vulnerability that resulted from doing this writing practice. Compared to how you were when you started this journey, give an example of lowered inhibitions or increased openness.

- Write about an area of your life where you lack freedom. What blocks you from taking this freedom now? How might freeing yourself in this area change you?

- Where do you feel blocked in your writing practice? Where do you hold back? What prevents you from telling the truth in writing?

- Revisit a setback to freedom in writing that you may have experienced on this journey. Which of your demons stopped you? What were you afraid to see? How were you able to get past this fear? If you have not done so, write about the block itself. What are the stories and beliefs behind it?

Freedom is part of your birthright as an individual. Having examined so many imprisoning stories, and used writing as a doorway to freedom, you now know that the moments when you do have setbacks—and seem to be back where you started—often coincide with the arrival of insight. Liberation is waiting around the bend. Along with freedom, flourishing comes. The purpose of this journey is to awaken you to new potentials that lead to your creative harvest, and bring you to a time to reap.

A TIME TO REAP

The purpose of planting is to reap. The reason for doing the hard work of writing is to bear the fruit of self-realization. With each seed of truth you've laid down in this process, some wisdom has taken root. As you practiced, these seedlings have pushed toward the light. Each time you sat down to write, you nourished the roots of awakening through self-inquiry and insight. The more you opened, the more you grew; the more you embody, the more you reap. This harvest will only increase if you continue to practice with each passing year.

This awakening process is both organic and spiritual. Just as nothing on earth grows without sunlight, your inner life cannot blossom without focused attention. This power of self-awareness connects us to one another, and sustains the cosmos. When you write—or engage in creativity of any kind—this energy is intensified.

You realize how much time you've wasted not telling the truth, struggling to avoid your own pain. This resistance blocked your own fruition, but now this self-sabotage is losing its strength. There are still days when you lose touch with your emotional truth but they're probably few, and farther between. Your fictions are losing their hold on you. You're no longer telling yourself stories in order to live. You're living mindfully in order to see through your stories.

That's the harvest I'm talking about. When this happened for me, I did not see it coming. I'd spent my life as a mainstream writer, but although I published a lot, there was nothing transformative about my work. Then my life fell apart. I almost died, my life myth was obliterated, and in the free-fall of catastrophe, with nowhere else to turn, I dove into my writing—and myself—in a different way. Writing, along with meditation and self-inquiry, brought about a kind of conversion. I realized there was a world inside me I had never looked at before. The more I dug down, the more I uncovered. Self-inquiry turned the soil, writing in detail planted the seeds, and reading what I'd written afterward brought the specimen to flower.

If I'd hadn't undergone this conversion myself, *Writing to Awaken* would never have happened. If I hadn't been forced to let go of my story, I might never have bothered to look underneath. Without loss, insecurity, pain, or fear—the nutrients of spiritual and creative progress—few would topple their own self-image and shovel around in the dark. Luckily, things do fall apart, and the opportunity for transformation does present itself. Writing gives us courage to welcome these changes and meet adversity with open eyes.

It's not that we're glad when bad things happen, but we recognize the potential latent in loss or catastrophe—a word that has a Greek root, meaning "to turn around." We understand that impermanence plays a positive role in our evolution, provided we don't run away from its lessons, or waste the chance to get free. Writing is your greatest ally in this, the helpmate that never leaves you. By continuing to ask yourself questions and reflect on the answers, you never need to feel powerless again. No matter how out of control life seems, you can always write your way back to center.

Karen did not completely believe this. Halfway through a nine-month class that focused on emotional and spiritual healing, Karen was diagnosed with cancer that threatened to end her life within the year. She had come to the class hoping to understand why she had trouble with intimate relationships, and had done remarkable, sometimes painful, writing about her history with romantic rejection. Karen had doubts about her physical attractiveness and was still grieving the end of her marriage after her husband left her for a younger woman. A shy, introverted middle-aged woman, Karen had been surprising herself as a writer, describing experiences, feelings, and beliefs she hadn't dared to express before. "I feel like I'm healing," she wrote a few months into the course. "There's a little light at the end of the tunnel."

After she got her diagnosis, Karen wrote a moving note to explain that she was dropping the course to focus on treatments and to prepare for what might be coming. I encouraged her to keep writing and invited Karen to follow the course at her own pace and send me work whenever she wanted. She accepted my offer gratefully but doubted that she would be able to write. "I need to take care of business," she told me. I reminded her that writing was serious business and suggested that she not underestimate how it might help her during this time.

I heard nothing from Karen for half a year. Then I received a letter to our class that came as a great relief and also confirmed what I knew about writing: that every time you practice, it makes you stronger, even when you're not aware of it.

> Dear Fellow Writers: I didn't want to disappear without telling you what had happened to me. These past months have been among the happiest in my entire life, which seems impossible but I swear is true. The news from my doctor isn't great. The cancer is taking its course and we're trying to slow it down with noninvasive treatments, but who knows? I'm focusing on healing, not curing. Which means that however long I have to live, I want to live it as a whole person. This writing showed me how un-whole I've felt for so much of my life. Like I didn't really know myself. But that's not my story anymore. When I look inside myself

these days, I feel like I'm being carried. All these months of writing were like sewing some kind of parachute. And now that I need it, it's there for me. I'm not crashing the way I expected to.

It's not that being sick doesn't suck but I don't feel the same kind of despair because I don't feel so alone anymore. I'm not flying solo; my writing is with me. I didn't even know it had helped me so much. Amazing. So I'm here to tell you: don't give up. You may not know that you're sewing this parachute for yourself, but you are. Just keep going.

Karen's letter was a powerful reminder that if we do the work, we will reap the rewards and those benefits will come to sustain us, especially in challenging times, moments when we most need to be reminded of who we are and what truly matters. The harvests of insight and strength are within you. They'll sustain you in remarkable ways. Writing will always help you to do this. You just need to keep showing up.

Core Insights

☐ The purpose of this writing practice is to bear the fruit of self-realization. With each seed of truth laid down in this process, some wisdom has taken root. Each time we sit down to write, we nourish the roots, and the harvest will increase if we continue the writing practice.

☐ The power of self-awareness connects us to one another, and sustains the cosmos.

☐ The more we open, the more we grow; the more we sow, the more we reap.

☐ When things fall apart, an opportunity for transformation will present itself. Writing gives us courage to welcome change and meet adversity with an open heart and an open mind.

Dive Deeper

The harvest of wisdom is beyond measure. Having planted the seeds of insight through writing, you continue to reap its rich rewards. These questions will help you unearth your findings and figure out how to put them to use. Once that happens, you'll realize there's nothing to do but begin again.

- What seeds of wisdom have taken root for you through this process? Which are still germinating and which have produced nothing? Why do you think that is?

- Write about how the process of self-exploration has connected you to a higher purpose and a more truthful path.

- Describe a catastrophic experience in your life. Were you able to see the opportunity for change at the time? Do you see it now? Explain.

- Do you use writing as source of centering? Do you feel the effects immediately or do they take time to develop and reveal themselves? Be specific.

Awakening is an organic process. You plant, reap, and plant again. You revisit the field you've plowed before and watch a new crop of insights break through, reaching toward the light of awareness. This natural cycle does not end as long as you cultivate a thriving practice. In our final lesson, we bless this process and learn to begin again.

THE ROAD AHEAD

At the end of our journey, we recognize that awakening never ends. Like all forms of spiritual practice, writing is about starting over. Every time you return to your desk, you discover new contours, details, and expressions, and bring fresh perspective to who you know yourself to be.

If you practice writing regularly, it will also help to keep you rooted in the present moment. The page reminds you that the past is dead and gone, and today is a whole new encounter. Studying your inner world makes everyday life evolutionary. You're reminded again and again that no single story could ever define you since you are always changing. No matter how many times you've abandoned your practice, or failed to meet your own expectations, it doesn't matter as long as you find your way back to the page. This act of returning is automatically inspirational. A meditation teacher I know puts it this way: "Every time you notice that your mind has wandered, and bring your attention back to the breath, that is a moment of enlightenment."

Showing up for your writing practice takes commitment and courage. People who don't write regularly rarely understand this. Why should they? Sitting down with pen and paper or keyboard hardly looks heroic from the outside, with your slippers on and a mug of tea by your side. But it takes a lot of chutzpah not to give up, not to stop growing. It calls on the seeker's spirit inside you. Most people who are attracted to expressive writing are individuals driven toward self-knowledge, drawn to look below the surface of their lives. This inexorable pull to know yourself fuels the writing process itself. Regardless of how much you already know, there's always a whole lot left to learn.

A longtime student of mine embodies this spirit of curiosity with brio. At eighty-two, Fern is a great survivor. A painter by profession, Fern is an Austrian Jew who came through two world wars, the loss of her country, the death of her husband, two heart attacks, the loss of a grandchild, and more psychological challenges than any single person I've ever known. For the past five years, without fail, Fern registers for the same online class. She follows the same sequence of lessons, responds to the same writing prompts, and brings the same level of curiosity and enthusiasm to each encounter with this curriculum. As Fern gets older and learns more about herself, her responses change from one year to the next. Half joking, I recently asked Fern why she doesn't try a new class. Her written response was enlightening.

> *Whenever I write, I feel more alive. Even when it's hard, I come away with more of myself—things I'd forgotten, the lost pieces. It's an ongoing education for me. Even though I'm using the same questions, I hear them differently every year. And your responses are always different. This is a mirror for how much I'm actually changing. I do this because it helps me keep a record of my inner journey. My journey, which belongs to me and nobody else. You know why Cezanne painted that same mountain more than twenty times? Because that was his work to do, it was teaching him how to see. It didn't matter how accomplished he was, Cezanne was always learning. Always beginning. It's the same thing with life. You can't step into the same river twice. Writing reminds me that now is now, a completely unique moment that will never come again in all of eternity. Isn't that the most amazing thing? The thing you never want to forget!*

Fern is extraordinary in her own way. The same goes for you. When you bring your Beginner's Mind and spirit to your writing, loving the practice for itself, no two days are ever the same. No two responses are identical, even when you're answering the same question. The page will always surprise you. You'll continue to learn and sharpen your eye, your heart will grow larger, your thoughts more expansive. The roar you once swallowed will echo and deepen, in writing and in life. You'll begin anew every time you write, and that will keep your practice fresh as this journey continues.

Core Insights

- ☐ Like all forms of spiritual practice, writing is always beginning anew. It is an opportunity to bring fresh perspective to who we know ourselves to be.

- ☐ Writing practiced regularly helps keep us honest and rooted in the present moment.

- ☐ Studying our inner world makes everyday life evolutionary.

- ☐ Writing reminds us that *now is now*, a completely unique moment that will never come again in all of eternity.

Dive Deeper

When you're ready to work through these final questions, bring everything you've learned to the page. Push your boundaries, guided by the Witness, and don't hold anything back.

- What will be the most challenging part of cultivating your ongoing writing practice? What is your plan for overcoming this difficulty?

- Take a week to reread your responses to the prompts in this book. Then write about the transformations you see. Is there an overarching theme that emerges? A story that still needs exploring? A breakthrough you never expected?

- What will your daily writing practice look like? What subjects will you focus on and why?

- How do you feel about starting over? Remaining a beginner in life and writing? How might this enrich your transformation? What might remain to be discovered?

When you tell the truth, your story changes.

When your story changes, your life is transformed.

Then you can begin again.

Acknowledgments

To my wonderful students: thank you for allowing me to share these stories. Your creativity, passion, and courage inspire me every day. Deep bows to Joy Harris, Sharyl Volpe, Rena Graham, Ryan Buresh, Clancy Drake, and Jennifer Holder for helping to bring this book into the world. And to David Moore, my phenomenal partner. Nothing happens without you.

Bibliography

Abram, Jan. *The Language of Winnicott.* London: Karnac Books, 2007.

Armstrong, Karen. "Man Versus God," *The Wall Street Journal.* September 12, 2009.

Baudelaire, Charles. *The Painter of Modern Life and Other Essays.* London: Phaidon Press, 1995.

Bly, Robert. *A Little Book on the Human Shadow.* San Francisco: Harper One, 1988.

Brown, Brené. *Daring Greatly.* New York: Penguin Press, 2012.

Buber, Martin. *The Legend of the Baal-Shem.* Princeton, NJ: Princeton University Press, 1995.

De Mille, Agness. *Martha: The Life and Work of Martha Graham.* New York: Random House, 1991.

Frankl, Viktor. *Man's Search for Meaning.* Boston: Beacon Press, 2006.

Fromm, Erich. *The Anatomy of Human Destructiveness.* New York: Henry Holt, 1973.

Gittings, Robert, ed. *John Keats: Selected Letters.* New York: Oxford University Press, 2002.

Hillman, James. *The Soul's Code.* New York: Warner Books, 1996.

Joyce, James. *Stephen Hero.* New York: New Directions, 1963.

Jung, C. G. "The Problem of Evil Today." *Meeting the Shadow: The Hidden Power of the Dark Side of Human Nature.* Connie Zweig, ed. New York: Jeremy Tarcher, 1991.

Jung, C. G. *Alchemical Studies (The Collected Works of C. G. Jung: Vol. 13).* Princeton, NJ: Princeton University Press, 1967.

Klein, Daniel. *Travels with Epicurus*. New York: Penguin Books, 2012.

Lewis, C. S. *The Inner Ring*. Oakland: C. S. Lewis Society of California, 1916.

Matousek, Mark. *Sex Death Enlightenment*. New York: Riverhead, 1996.

Nietzsche, Friedrich Wilhelm. *Thus Spake Zarathustra*. New York: Oxford University Press, 2005.

Pennebaker, James W. *Opening Up*. New York: The Guilford Press, 1997.

Perel, Esther. *Mating in Captivity*. New York: Harper Collins, 2006.

Roethke, Theodore. *The Collected Poems of Theodore Roethke*. New York: Doubleday, 1961.

Russell, Bertrand. *In Praise of Idleness and Other Essays*. New York: Touchstone, 1972.

Siebert, Al. *The Survivor Personality*. New York: Berkley Publishing Group, 1996.

Siegel, Daniel J. *The Developing Mind*. New York: Guildford Press, 2012.

Suzuki, Shunryu. *Zen Mind, Beginner's Mind*. Boston: Shambhala Publications, 2006.

Tagore, Rabindranath. *The English Writings of Rabindranath Tagore: Vol. 1*. Sisir Kumar Das, ed. New Delhi: Suhitya Akademi, 2004.

Thomas, Dylan. *The Poems of Dylan Thomas*. New York: New Directions, 2003.

Tolle, Eckhart. *The Power of Now*. Vancouver: Namaste Publishing, 2004.

Whitman, Walt. *Leaves of Grass*. Mineola, NY: Dover Publications, 2007.

Mark Matousek is author of two award-winning memoirs, *Sex Death Enlightenment* (an international bestseller) and *The Boy He Left Behind* (a *Los Angeles Times* Discovery Book), as well as *When You're Falling, Dive* and *Ethical Wisdom*. He collaborated with Sogyal Rinpoche on *The Tibetan Book of Living and Dying*, Andrew Harvey on *Dialogues with a Modern Mystic*, and Ram Dass on *Still Here*. Matousek is a featured blogger for *Psychology Today, The Huffington Post*, and *Contemplative Journal*, and has contributed to numerous anthologies and publications, including *The New Yorker, O, The Oprah Magazine* (as a contributing editor), *The New York Times Magazine, Harper's BAZAAR, Yoga Journal, Details, The Saturday Evening Post, AARP, Tricycle*, and more. A popular lecturer and writing teacher, he is on the faculty of the New York Open Center, the Esalen Institute, Hollyhock, and Schumacher College. Matousek is also creative director of V-Men (with Eve Ensler), an organization devoted to ending violence against women and girls. His workshops, classes, and mentoring have helped thousands of people around the world, focusing on personal awakening and creative excellence through self-inquiry and writing.

Foreword writer **Joan Borysenko, PhD**, is a pioneer in the integration of mind, body, and spirit. She is a licensed psychologist with a doctorate in cell biology from Harvard Medical School, and president of Mind-Body Health Sciences. A *New York Times* bestselling author of sixteen books and several meditation CDs, Borysenko synthesizes cutting-edge science with deep humanity.

MORE BOOKS for the SPIRITUAL SEEKER

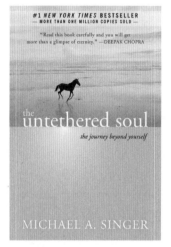

ISBN: 978-1572245372 | US $16.95

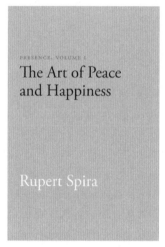

ISBN: 978-1626258747 | US $19.95

ISBN: 978-1908664396 | US $16.95

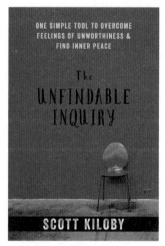

ISBN: 978-1626258129 | US $16.95

 newharbingerpublications

 NON-DUALITY PRESS | SAHAJA | REVEAL PRESS